ROUGH GUIDES

ROUGH GUIDES WALKS & TOURS

SRI LANKA

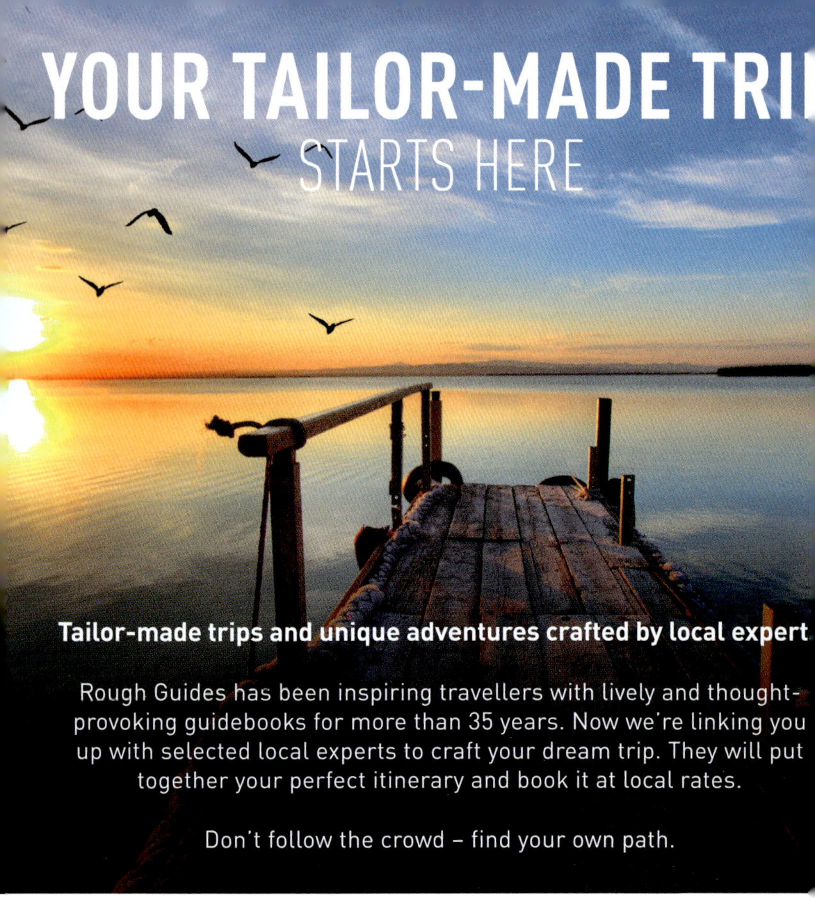

YOUR TAILOR-MADE TRI STARTS HERE

Tailor-made trips and unique adventures crafted by local expert

Rough Guides has been inspiring travellers with lively and thought-provoking guidebooks for more than 35 years. Now we're linking you up with selected local experts to craft your dream trip. They will put together your perfect itinerary and book it at local rates.

Don't follow the crowd – find your own path.

HOW ROUGHGUIDES.COM/TRIPS WORKS

STEP 1

Pick your dream destination, tell us what you want and submit an enquiry.

STEP 2

Fill in a short form to tell your local expert about your dream trip and preferences.

STEP 3

Our local expert will craft your tailor-made itinerary. You'll be able to tweak and refine it until you're completely satisfied.

STEP 4

Book online with ease, pack your bags and enjoy the trip! Our local expert will be on hand 24/7 while you're on the road.

BENEFITS OF PLANNING AND BOOKING AT ROUGHGUIDES.COM/TRIPS

PLAN YOUR ADVENTURE WITH LOCAL EXPERTS

Rough Guides' English-speaking local experts are hand-picked, based on their experience in the travel industry and their impeccable standards of customer service.

SAVE TIME AND GET ACCESS TO LOCAL KNOWLEDGE

When a local expert plans your trip, you save time and money when you book, even during high season. You won't be charged for using a credit card either.

MAKE TRAVEL A BREEZE: BOOK WITH PEACE OF MIND

Enjoy stress-free travel when you use Rough Guides' secure online booking platform. All bookings come with a money-back guarantee.

WHAT DO OTHER TRAVELLERS THINK ABOUT ROUGH GUIDES TRIPS?

Trip to Spain

This Spain tour company did a fantastic job to make our dream trip perfect. We gave them our travel budget, told them where we would like to go, and they did all of the planning. Our drivers and tour guides were always on time and very knowledgable. The hotel accommodations were better than we would have found on our own. Only one time did we end up in a location that we had not intended to be in. We called the 24 hour phone number, and they immediately fixed the situation.

Don A, USA ★★★★★

Trip to Morocco

Our trip was fantastic! Transportation, accommodations, guides – all were well chosen! The hotels were well situated, well appointed and had helpful, friendly staff. All of the guides we had were very knowledgeable, patient, and flexible with our varied interests in the different sites. We particularly enjoyed the side trip to Tangier! Well done! The itinerary you arranged for us allowed maximum coverage of the country with time in each city for seeing the important places.

Sharon, USA ★★★★★

PLAN AND BOOK YOUR TRIP AT ROUGHGUIDES.COM/TRIPS

CONTENTS

Introduction

Trip plans

Directory

Ancient temples

Marvel at the Cultural Triangle's ancient shrines and stupas (tours 7 and 8), pay homage at the revered Temple of the Tooth (tour 4) or visit the eclectic Gangaramaya temple in Colombo (tour 2).

Best Walks & Tours for...

Animal lovers

Watch the magnificent Gathering of the Elephants at Minneriya (tour 8), go searching for elusive leopards in Yala and Kumana (tours 11 and 12) or go on a night-time turtle-watch at Rekawa (tour 10).

Beaches

Laze on Negombo's sandy seafront (tour 3), head to the popular backpacker village at Unawatuna (walk 9) or make for the remote east-coast beaches around Arugam Bay (tour 12).

Botanical gardens

Get back to nature at Sri Lanka's stunning botanical gardens (tours 4 and 5) or explore the dry-zone jungle of the pristine Popham Arboretum (tour 7).

Colonial architecture

Discover ornate British buildings in Colombo Fort (walk 1), the grand old colonial hotels of Nuwara Eliya (tour 5) or wander the time-warp of the Dutch-era streets and ramparts of Galle Fort (walk 9).

Hottest curries

If hotel food is too bland, search for spicier cuisine in the restaurants of Kandy (tour 4), Colombo (tour 2), and Ella (tour 6), where you'll find a wide spread of restaurants.

Mountain views

Peer through Ella Gap for fabulous views down to the south coast (tour 6), glimpse Mount Pidurutalagala, Sri Lanka's highest peak, from Nuwara Eliya (tour 5); or scramble up to Lipton's Seat (tour 6) for breathtaking vistas.

Tea trekking

Trek through tea gardens to your heart's content at Kandapola (tour 5) and Haputale (tour 6), relishing the cool mountain air, then warm up with a cup of pure Ceylon tea in a plantation bungalow.

INTRODUCTION

An introduction to Sri Lanka and what makes it special, what not to miss and what to do when you're there.

Discover Sri Lanka

Sri Lanka is one of Asia's ultimate island paradises, with endless miles of golden beaches and verdant tropical landscapes. But the island also boasts a remarkable physical, cultural and ethnic diversity, as well as a long and dramatic history.

The shape of Sri Lanka on the map has been compared to many things: a teardrop falling from the tip of India, a pearl, a mango and (to Dutch colonists) a leg of ham. Tears were for many years the island's dominant emotion, the result of 26 years of devastating civil war which blighted the island's recent history until the conclusion of hostilities in 2009. Sri Lanka's tourism industry boomed over the decade which followed the end of the war, establishing the island as one of the Indian Ocean's go-to destinations thanks to its remarkably varied array of attractions including idyllic beaches, ancient cultural spectacles, dramatic landscapes and rich wildlife. The devastating economic crisis which hit the country during 2019 may have undone some of Sri Lanka's hard-won recent gains, although as of 2024 visitor numbers had revived to previous levels and the island was once again looking to the future with optimism.

Geography and layout

Sri Lanka is a small country: a modest 435km (271 miles) from top to bottom, and 240km (149 miles) from east to west. Lying a few degrees north of the Equator in the balmy waters of the Indian Ocean, the island has an incredibly diverse range of landscapes, from the sultry tropical beaches, coconut plantations and lowland jungles of the coast to the cool green hill country with its mist-shrouded mountains, crashing waterfalls and endless tea plantations.

Exploring the country

The island's relatively small size and good road and rail infrastructure mean that it's possible to see many of the island's highlights in just a few days, although distances can sometimes be deceptive – congested roads around major towns and challenging topography in the hill country can make drives which look short on the map take rather longer than you might expect. The starting point for most visitors is the either the capital, Colombo or the beach resort of Negombo, a short ride from the international airport. Colombo itself is easily explored either on foot or by hiring one of the motorised rickshaws (tuk-tuks) which can be seen everywhere across the island.

Colombo is also the starting point for the fine journey by road (or rail)

Train travel through the tea plantations

to Sri Lanka's cultural capital, Kandy. From Kandy you can drive north to the ancient ruined cities and great Buddhist monuments of the Cultural Triangle. Alternatively, head south from Kandy to explore the verdant tea plantations, spectacular scenery and engaging old colonial mementoes of the island's breezy hill country and then continue on to Yala National Park in the south before returning to Colombo via Tangalla and Galle. Alternatively, head north from Yala and head to remote Arugam Bay, the east coast's most appealing destination.

Many visitors also spend some time on one of Sri Lanka's west-coast beaches; resort areas (all easily reached from Colombo or Galle) include Bentota, Beruwala and Hikkaduwa. While this area is lighter on sights than elsewhere, the miles of golden, sun-kissed sand and some idyllic places to stay (see page 91) make this a hugely popular choice for sun-starved European visitors, whether for a two-week package holiday or for some R'n'R during a wider tour of the country.

History

The first humans to arrive in Sri Lanka were the aboriginal Veddhas, who walked across from India around 16,000 BC. Around the fourth century BC, immigrants from both North and South India – the ancestors of Sri Lanka's modern Sinhalese and Tamils – began to arrive.

Gangaramaya Temple, Colombo

Early development of the island was mainly in the northern half, where the ancient ruins of Anuradhapura and Polonnaruwa testify to a glorious Buddhist culture and pioneering agricultural development, including the creation of huge reservoirs (tanks) and a staggeringly elaborate network of waterways and irrigation works.

After the thirteenth century, the island became politically fragmented, with the inland Kingdom of Kandy vying for power with a series of smaller statelets in the south. The sixteenth century also saw the arrival of the Portuguese, ushering in the long colonial period during which the island would change hands between no less than three European powers.

The Portuguese gradually seized control of most of the island – apart

New Kathiresan Kovil Temple

Winds of fortune

The trade winds, on which the monsoons are carried to Sri Lanka, not only keep the island watered but also helped make it rich. In former centuries the winds provided a reliable shuttle service for traders from Greece, China, Arabia and Rome searching for spices and gems. Since these seafaring merchants had to wait for the winds to change direction before they could sail home, many decided to stay and set up business instead, developing the island's trade.

from the remote, inland Kingdom of Kandy – before losing the island to the Dutch in 1656. The Dutch made fortunes trading on the island's spices, cinnamon, elephants and precious gemstones before being displaced at the start of the nineteenth century by the British, who gave the island the railways, roads, tea plantations and parliamentary democracy which survive largely unchanged to this day.

Independence finally arrived in 1948, although Sri Lanka's post-colonial history was shaped by violent tensions between the island's majority Sinhalese and minority Tamil populations, leading to a bloody 26-year civil war which raged from 1983 to 2009 between government forces and the rebel LTTE (Liberation Tigers of Tamil Eelam – or Tamil Tigers, as they're usually called). Many lives were also lost in 2004, when Sri Lanka was hit by the catastrophic Asian tsunami.

After a decade of peace and rising prosperity, further turmoil arrived in 2019, when the island plunged into a major economic crisis, massively exacerbated by the arrival of Covid a year later. Recovery has been slow and painful, although as of 2024 the island's finances have significantly recovered and the country is looking once more to the future with renewed – if cautious – optimism.

Climate

The island's climate is so diverse it's possible to travel in just a few hours from the tropical heat of the coast to the cool and misty uplands of the hill country – to start the day sweating and end it shivering. There are two separate monsoon seasons, one in the east, the other in the southwest. The climate along the west coast is best from December to April, while the best weather on the east coast is from May to October. Expect high humidity and temperatures on the coast of around 27°C (81°F). Kandy, at 305m (1,000ft), averages 20°C (68°F), and Nuwara Eliya, at 1,890m (6,200ft), just 16°C (61°F).

Population

Tensions between Sri Lanka's varied ethnic groups – most notably Sinhalese and Tamils – have been a feature of

A traditional boat off Unawatuna Beach

island life for over two thousand years, resulting in one of modern Asia's longest and bloodiest civil wars but also giving the island its uniquely varied cultural flavour. Interracial rivalry is fought out with games of 'we got here first', with both Sinhalese and Tamils arguing about precedence. The British colonial period led to the introduction of English as a link language between the Tamils and the Sinhalese, but this link was lost when S.W.R.D

Don't leave Sri Lanka without...

Climbing to the top of Sigiriya. Ascending this unforgettable rock-fortress, one of Sri Lanka's most dramatic natural sights, gives you incredible views over the surrounding plains. See page 65.

Hitting the beach. Sri Lanka's coast is fringed with sun-soaked golden beaches and luscious palm trees; if you're short for time, head to Negombo, just half an hour from Colombo airport. See page 40.

Paying homage to the tooth. Kandy's Temple of the Tooth is Sri Lanka's most important pilgrimage site. Time your visit right and you'll be rewarded with a glimpse of the golden casket containing the Buddha's Tooth Relic. See page 44.

Sampling hoppers. A Sri Lankan breakfast staple, also found at many street cafés, these delicate little bowl-shaped pancakes are great on their own, eaten with curry or cooked with an egg in the centre. See page 17.

Catching a Kandyan dance show. Spectacularly costumed dancers perform acrobatic choreography to an insistent accompaniment of high-octane drumming. See page 45.

Visiting a tea plantation. Travel past spectacular waterfalls, verdant hills lined with tea terraces and roadside fruit sellers to reach Sri Lanka's working tea plantations, where you can have a brew and learn all about the process from plant to cup. See page 49.

Catching a cricket match. Join the crowds at a test or one-day match for an insight into Sri Lanka's other major religion: cricket. See page 24.

Taking in the view at Ella Gap. The staggering view from Ella Gap, in a charming hill country village, takes in miles of peaks, valleys and – on a clear day – the southern plateau all the way to the coast. See page 58.

Learning about Ayurveda. Ayurvedic wellness centres are found everywhere and even if you're not looking for a specific cure, the natural science behind it is fascinating to discover. See page 25.

Spotting leopards. Tracking down this elusive big cat at Yala National Park is an experience even if you don't manage a sighting, with elephants, wild boar and more to keep you diverted. See page 82.

Transport in Galle

Worshippers at the sacred Sri Maha Bodhi

Bandaranaike made Sinhala the official language. Tamils found their aspirations thwarted unless they learned Sinhala.

Around three-quarters of the island's population is Sinhalese Buddhist, whose ancestors migrated to Sri Lanka from North India around the fourth century BC. The Tamils are Sri Lanka's second-largest ethnic group, comprising around 15 percent of the population (of which some four percent are descendants of immigrants brought over from India by the British to work in the island's tea plantations). Most Sri Lankan Tamils are Hindus, although there are also many Tamil Christians.

Sri Lanka's Muslims (around 9 percent of the population) have been living on the island for over a millennium, having arrived as merchants, and now mostly live on the east coast. One of the island's smallest but most colourful ethnic groups is the Burghers – white, English-speaking Sri Lankans descended from European settlers, mainly Dutch and Portuguese.

The population is mainly rural (about 80 percent), although since vast tracks of mountainous jungle and arid plains are largely uninhabited, the population density is high in settled areas around the coast, and particularly in the major cities.

Local customs

Most Sri Lankans are generally exceptionally friendly and helpful. They also place great emphasis on politeness and manners, as exemplified by the fabulously courteous staff at top-end hotels – raising your voice in a dispute is usually counterproductive.

Nudity and toplessness are not permitted on any Sri Lankan beaches, and overt physical displays of affection in public are also frowned upon – Sri Lankan couples hide behind enormous umbrellas in the quiet corners of parks and botanical gardens.

People are usually happy to have their photo taken, but always ask first. And note that the island's famously picturesque stilt fishermen usually expect payment in return for a picture.

All visitors to Buddhist and Hindu temples should be appropriately dressed. You should never have yourself photographed (or take a selfie) posing with a Buddha image – that is, with your back to the image.

For more on etiquette, see page 107.

Politics

Sri Lanka has been a parliamentary democracy since independence in 1948, headed by an elected executive president. The island's two major parties are the centre-right, business-oriented United National Party (UNP) and the more conservative, Buddhist-nationalist Sri Lanka Freedom Party (SLFP). Power has flipped regularly between these two parties since 1948, often involving

Kandyan dancing

Top tips for exploring Sri Lanka

Travel visa. Visitors to Sri Lanka should obtain an Electronic Travel Authorisation (ETA) before they travel (www.srilankaevisa.lk). This allows tourist entry for up to 30 days, for US$50. Visas can be extended to three months at the Immigration Service Centre in Colombo.

Staying healthy. Sri Lanka was declared free of malaria by the WHO in 2016 – a remarkable public health achievement. The mosquito-borne dengue fever, however, remains a genuine risk, particularly in Colombo and along the west coast, following the southwest monsoon (Oct/Nov). There's no vaccine, so do your best to avoid being bitten.

Sun and heat. Sunburn and sunstroke are a risk in lowland Sri Lanka, whether you're lying on the beach or exploring ancient monuments. An umbrella is never out of place, both for warding off rain and sheltering from the sun.

Safe swimming. Drowning is a leading cause of tourist deaths in Sri Lanka, and swimming in certain places around the coast can be dangerous due to strong currents and riptides. Always check locally before getting into the water, and never swim while under the influence.

Tuk-tuk touting. Tuk-tuk drivers can't bear to see foreigners walking. A polite shake of the head (and avoid making eye contact) usually works. If you do want a ride, be sure to agree a fare before setting off. It's worth checking at your guesthouse or hotel beforehand to get an idea of how much the fare should be, although you'll need to accept that as a foreigner you will pretty much always pay a bit more than the locals.

complex coalition arrangements including an array of smaller parties, most notably the populist JVP.

The country's healthy democratic traditions were seriously threatened under the quasi-dictatorial regime of former leader Mahinda Rajapakse, who allegedly attempted to quash the results of the 2015 presidential election after falling to defeat. Leading figures from the army, police and judiciary are said to have been pressured to overturn the result in an attempted coup. All three, mercifully, told Rajapakse to get lost.

Economics

The top foreign-exchange earners are the manufacture of garments exported to the West, inward remittances from Sri Lankans working overseas, mainly in the Gulf, and revenues from tourism. The island's tea industry also continues to account for a healthy slice of the export trade, at around 17 percent.

The people of Sri Lanka enjoy free education and healthcare, and a literacy rate of 92 percent – one of the highest in Asia and the highest in South Asia.

Travelling by tuk-tuk

Women working in the tea plantations

Food and Drink

Sri Lankan cuisine may not be renowned beyond the island's shores, but it features a distinctive and delicious blend of flavours based on local ingredients and spices, from the heat of chillies to the sweetness of coconuts.

Far more than a variation on the classic cuisines of neighbouring India, Sri Lankan cooking has its own unique set of flavours, inspired by the island's abundant natural produce and the huge variety of spices grown locally. Rice and curry remains culinary king, but with fiercer flavours than in India and with sauces based on coconut milk and fiery chilli sambols, making it closer to Thai cooking in style.

Over the centuries, Sri Lanka's visitors and invaders have contributed Indian, Chinese, Malay and Arab influences, as well as Portuguese, Dutch and British dishes. In hotel buffets you might encounter all of them at the same time, so take the chance to sample what Sri Lanka can offer – rare spices, unusual vegetables, tropical fruits and some of the world's fattest prawns, not to mention the classic Sri Lankan rice and curry, a miniature banquet all on its own.

Local cuisine

Sri Lankan food has a reputation for being deliciously hot, thanks to the use of generous quantities of chillies and other warming spices. Sri Lankan cooks don't reach for a packet of curry powder but instead spend hours grinding selected spices to create a dish that is rich in flavour as well as pungent – a good cook can spend hours preparing an authentic curry. While Sri Lankans have been raised to expect their curries to be hot, visitors may be served milder versions, tamed by the addition of coconut milk.

The method of preparation has evolved over the centuries. The abundance of fresh vegetables (some introduced by the British in the nineteenth century) and forest roots, as well as locally grown spices like cardamom, cinnamon, cloves and curry leaves (*karapincha*) contribute to making Sri Lankan curries special. This small green leaf adds a distinctive flavour with an aroma akin to lime and sesame when crushed, and also has the reputation of being good for lowering cholesterol.

Curries are flavoured with different spices to match the main ingredient. Meat or fish, and vegetables like eggplant, cabbage, beans and even pineapple, lend themselves to hot curries. Root vegetables and cashew

A traditional Sri Lankan breakfast

You won't go short of rice and curry

nuts work better as mild curries. Curries cooked in the traditional way – in a clay pot over a wood fire – take on spicier flavours, thanks to the time taken to cook them.

Rice is the staple, and there are over 15 varieties in Sri Lanka. A favourite is the red country rice, *kakuluhaal*. This strain is full of vitamins and has a nutty flavour, as the grains are left unpolished. White rice, whether the ball-shaped *sambha*, the long-grained *basmati* or the white *milchard*, is widely available.

Rice and curry meals, served at the table in bowls or at buffets, always have the meat or fish curries cooked and served separately from the vegetable curries, so vegetarians can select what to eat without qualms.

Breakfast

Appa (hoppers), a type of pancake with crispy edges and made of rice flour or plain flour with coconut milk and yeast, is a favourite Sri Lankan breakfast dish. It can also be served with a fried egg nestling in it and is sensational when eaten with a beef curry and *seeni sambol*, a sweet, spicy onion relish.

Kiribath (milk rice) is a breakfast dish made with rice, cooked in coconut cream or fresh milk and spices. This is considered an auspicious meal and is eaten during special occasions – on the first of each month, or when welcoming visitors.

Lunch

Lunch packets of rice and curry (usually rice with three vegetable curries and one meat curry) are the mainstay of office workers. Packets are available in simple cafés and from street stalls throughout Colombo. When Sri Lankans travel, they typically lunch in rest houses, where a typical spread would consist of curries made of plantain, lentils, beef, fish, beans and eggplant, accompanied by bitter *gourd sambol* (a relish), *gotakola medun* (a leaf salad), devilled potatoes, a spicy mango chutney, and papadums served with fried red chillies and chunks of dry fish.

Dinner

For dinner at home, a Sri Lankan might have a curry served with *indiappa* (string hoppers), a Sri

Colourful ingredients that pack a punch

Lankan invention that resembles fine noodles. It is made by squeezing a mixture of rice flour (or plain flour) and water through a colander onto bamboo trays and then steam-cooking the mix until it's fluffy.

String-hopper *biriyani* – a lunch or dinner delicacy – is produced by breaking *indiappa* into small pieces and then cooking it with spices, meat and cashew nuts. *Lamprais* is a Dutch variation in which rice and curries are wrapped in banana leaves and steamed with chicken or beef.

'Devilled' dishes are also popular. These are usually prepared with a thick, spicy sauce plus big chunks of onion and chilli, though the end product often isn't as hot as you might fear (unless you eat all the chillies). Devilled chicken, pork, fish and beef are all common.

Other delicacies

Biriyani, a traditional Muslim rice-and-meat dish, and Tamil *dosas* (pancakes) and *vade* (fritters), have also become part of local cooking. *Pittu* is ground rice or plain flour mixed with coconut, steam-cooked in a bamboo container, and then eaten with coconut milk, or with meat or fish.

A kind of flimsy pancake, *godamba roti* is a particular favourite among Muslims. It is fascinating to see this being made: with each turn of the expert handler's wrist, a small ball of flour becomes longer and flatter.

Another popular dish is *watallappan*, a deliciously rich dessert concocted out of *jaggery* (a coarse brown sugar made from the sap of the date palm), eggs, milk and cashew nuts.

Snacks

Local snacks, known as 'short eats', consist of savoury bite-sized pastries or rolls which can be bought in pastry shops to eat in or take away. There are many types, including miniature loaves baked and stuffed with *seeni sambol*, fried pancakes with a beef, fish, chicken or vegetable filling, meat or chicken patties, and 'cutlets', deep-fried soft round balls of mashed tuna.

Fruit

The island's cornucopia of tropical fruits includes pineapple, passion fruit, pomegranate, papaya, avocados, mangoes, several kinds of guava, more than a dozen varieties of banana (including the much-loved sweet red bananas), and many more exotic offerings that will not be familiar from back home. Look out for the deep purple, delicately grape-flavoured mangosteen, star apples and the maverick *durian*, a huge green fruit whose pungent smell usually puts people off sampling its delicious, nougat-flavoured flesh. Even bigger than the durian is the *jak*, the world's largest fruit, which is eaten both raw and in cooked in curries.

String hoppers

Food and drink prices

Throughout this book, the below is a price guide for a meal for one:

$$$$ = over Rs5000
$$$ = Rs3000–5000
$$ = Rs1500–3000
$ = below Rs1500

Where to eat

Eating in the restaurant of your hotel or guesthouse is generally a safe bet: food turnover is usually high, as are standards of freshness and hygiene. That's where you will also be able to get non-spicy dishes like grilled fish or barbecued lobster. There will always be a choice, so you don't have to be like a Sri Lankan and have curry for every meal. Many of the island's numerous private villas and small boutique hotels also dish up superb food, although this is sometimes served only to in-house guests. The best restaurants for fusion, ethnic or continental fine dining are in Colombo. Some hotels away from the city also have good restaurants, which offer a break from stereotypical buffet food.

Village restaurants and eateries may prove testing due to the spicy food and suspect hygiene. Unlike other Asian countries, Sri Lanka has no tradition of street food. Rest houses are usually a safe bet for local food as they are used to catering for foreign travellers as well as for their usual clientele of lawyers, government officials and sales reps. A nice custom is for drivers of guests to eat free with the staff in hotels and guesthouses, so don't worry about inviting your chauffeur to join you for dinner.

Drinks

All imported beverages (wines, spirits and beers) carry a high tax, making them relatively expensive. Wine is readily available, including Australian, Chilean and South African vintages. The main locally brewed beer is Lion Lager, while you'll also find Anchor and locally brewed Carlsberg. For a taste of an authentic Sri Lankan product, try *arrack*, a feisty spirit, a bit like rum in both taste and strength, made from toddy (the sap of the coconut palm tree). Fresh, unfermented toddy is also much enjoyed by Sri Lankans, though its strong, sweaty aroma can be off-putting.

The sale of alcohol is prohibited on *Poya* (full moon) days, even to tourists staying in hotels, and on other days according to government decree. Buy your supplies the day before.

For teetotallers, there is tea, of course, as well as fruit juices, with fresh lime and soda being especially refreshing. A *thambili* (young coconut) cut open by a roadside vendor so you can drink the water within is a healthy natural beverage. Another local speciality is ginger beer made with real ginger (but make sure it's the Elephant House brand for that distinctive taste).

Preparing a king coconut for drinking

Watalappan

Shopping

Sri Lankan craftsmanship has a long and vibrant history, and although shops around the island serve up a fair amount of low-quality tourist tat, search a bit deeper and you'll find a great range of superior traditional and contemporary crafts to take home as a memento of your visit.

The quality of local craftsmanship in Sri Lanka declined following the mass influx of package tourists in the 1970s and 1980s, although standards have experienced something of a revival over the past decade or so, with a decent selection of more original and upmarket crafts now available. These often show the influence of the island's leading contemporary designers such as batik artist Ena de Silva and Barbara Sansoni, founder of the famous Barefoot shop in Colombo, whose vibrantly coloured textiles have become almost the trademark signature of modern Sri Lankan style.

Where to buy

Colombo is home to a number of classy boutiques including Odel (for fashion), Paradise Road (for superior homeware) and, especially, Barefoot, for its trademark fabrics, while shopping malls such as the upmarket Crescat (see tour 2) and the big new One Galle Face are also worth a look. The other main places to buy traditional crafts are Kandy, which has a deluge of craft shops, and Galle, famous for its gems, jewellery, lace and Dutch antiques, as well as a smattering of expat-owned designer boutiques.

For consumables, local supermarkets such as the island-wide Cargills chain offer another good – if not particularly exotic – hunting ground, usually carrying a good stock of local tea, spices and other local edibles at far cheaper prices than you'll find in hotel gift shops and the like.

Bargaining is the order of the day in smaller shops. A request for a 'small discount' or a 'special price' can sometimes work, especially if you're making a big purchase or buying several items.

Crafts

Probably Sri Lanka's most obvious collectibles are the colourful, and often faintly gruesome, *kolam* masks, found at shops all over the country. The centre of mask production is Ambalangoda, where there are a number of large shops selling a wide range of designs, some of heirloom quality.

Second in popularity are elephant carvings, ranging from garish little wooden creatures painted in bright

Batik design is an intricate process

polka-dot patterns to the elegant stone carvings sold at places like Paradise Road in Colombo. Batik, an art introduced by the Dutch from Indonesia, is also widespread. Batik designs are often stereotypical (the Sigiriya Damsels and naff beach scenes are ubiquitous), though a few places such as Jayamali Batiks in Kandy (www.jayamalibatiks.com) and Jez Look in Matara (www.facebook.com/jezbatik) produce more unusual and interesting work.

Lacquerware, a speciality of the Matale area, can also sometimes be found, along with Kandyan-style drums and, occasionally, carrom boards. Wooden models of tuk-tuks and other vehicles (most commonly found in Negombo) are another local speciality and make good souvenirs or children's toys, while you'll probably also see examples of the ingenious local puzzle boxes – impossible to open until you've been shown how.

Good places to buy traditional and contemporary crafts and other local items include the government-run Laksala chain (Bauddhaloka Mw, Colombo, plus other branches around the island), Barefoot and Paradise Road in Colombo, and the fun Luv SL chain (island-wide).

Gems

Sri Lanka has been famous for its gems since antiquity, including blue sapphires, star sapphires and star rubies, Alexandrites, Cat's Eye (named after the streak of light in its middle, like the eye of a cat), amethysts, garnets, aquamarines and moonstones. The biggest concentrations of gemshops are in Colombo and Galle. Only buy from reputable outfits such as Zam Gems (www.zamgems.com) and Sifani (www.sifani.com) or, in Galle, the long-running Laksana (www.facebook.com/laksanajewellery).

Tea and spices

There's a good selection of local teas and spices available in most branches of the island-wide Cargills supermarket chain or (at higher prices) from the various Mlesna tea shops. Unblended single-estate teas can be bought direct from many tea factories, while the Sri Lanka Tea Board shop on Galle Road in Kollupitiya, Colombo, also has an excellent selection.

Clothes

Sri Lanka is a major garment-manufacturing centre for overseas companies, and there are lots of good-quality Western-style clothes knocking around at bargain prices, as well as some good local labels. In Colombo, places to try include Odel (www.odel.lk) and Cotton Collection (www.facebook.com/cottoncollectionsl). Colourful but flimsy beachwear is flogged by shops and hawkers at all the major west coast resorts – it's cheap and cheerful, but don't expect it to last much longer than your holiday.

Gems galore

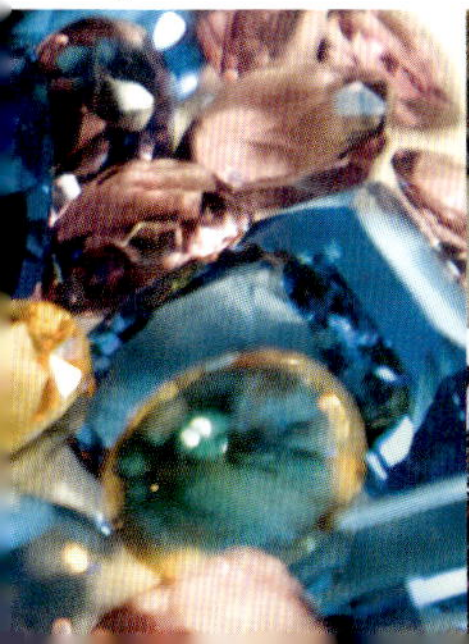

Woodcarvings

Entertainment

Entertainment in Sri Lanka very much reflects the island's cultural roots. Western-style nightlife is conspicuous by its general absence, but the island's packed calendar of exuberant religious festivals and performances of Kandyan drumming, dancing and other traditional entertainments more than compensate.

Festivals

The Sri Lankan calendar is studded with religious festivals, and with four major faiths on the island and no fewer than 25 public holidays, things can seem to grind to a halt with disconcerting frequency. Larger festivals include the Navam Perahera in Colombo (February), the Kataragama Festival (July/August) and – the grand-daddy of all Sri Lankan festivals – the Esala Perahera in Kandy (July/August). Larger festivals generally feature spectacular processions, caparisoned elephants, and drummers and dancers aplenty. The Sinhalese and Tamil New Year Festival in mid-April is another major event, when shops close and people visit their home villages, many to take part in contests like greasy pole pillow fights and bicycle races.

Non-religious festivals are much thinner on the ground, although the long-running Galle Literary Festival (Jan) has established an international reputation among bibliophiles.

Dance and music

The classical performing arts of Sri Lanka are generally divided into two groups: up-country, or Kandyan, encompassing the aristocratic classical dance traditions of the former Kandyan kingdom, with their lavishly costumed dancers and highly stylised choreography; and low-country, covering the much more populist traditions of the south. These feature masked *kolam* dance-dramas (usually a satirical portrayal of village life) and exorcism ceremonies, which still show strong pre-Buddhist roots and continue to be a vital part of Sri Lankan culture.

Performances of Kandyan drumming and dancing (usually incorporating a few low-country dances as well) are staged nightly at several venues in Kandy, while performers can also be seen out and about across the island dressed up in their finery, performing in hotel lobbies, for weddings, or just out in the street for the sheer fun of it. Fire dancers and performers walking over hot coals are other popular traditional entertainments you might catch a sight of – again, often staged for the benefit of guests at larger hotels.

Modern art in Colombo

Nightlife

If you want raucous after-dark nightlife, Sri Lanka generally isn't the place to come. There's a low-key club scene in Colombo itself, although specific venues come and go with baffling rapidity – check online to see where's new and cool.

For the island's best nightlife, the beach resorts are the places to go, particularly Unawatuna, Hikkaduwa and Arugam Bay, all of which host regular late-night beach parties with pumping music and partying on the sands. Other coastal resorts are a lot quieter, although you should at least find a couple of late-opening bars or restaurants with maybe a bit of a soundtrack, a view of the waves and a decent drinks list. Inland things are even quieter. There's a modicum of tourist-inspired nightlife in Ella, but that's about it – even Kandy, the country's second-largest city, is usually dead as a doornail by 10pm.

Performer on Negombo Beach

Art galleries and more

Regularly changing exhibitions of work by local artists are staged at Colombo's Gallery Café (www.paradiseroad.lk), the Saskia Fernando Gallery (www.saskiafernandogallery.com) and Barefoot (www.barefootceylon.com). Colombo's unofficial cultural hub, Barefoot also hosts a range of other events including live music performances and talks with eminent local creative types, while their regular Sunday afternoon jazz sessions have virtually become a city institution.

For more informal street art, check out the colourful open-air art 'gallery' on Green Path, near the Colombo National Museum, where local students and assorted part-time painters come to display their work, hanging canvases from the railings along the side of the road. All artworks on display are for sale, often at very affordable prices, and the quality is generally high. It's busiest at weekends, although there are sometimes a few paintings on display during the week as well.

Fire dancing is a typical hotel entertainment

Activities

From surfing, diving and white-water rafting through to a gentle yoga session or a spa treatment, Sri Lanka has activities for the energetic, as well as many pleasant ways to unwind.

Cricket

Cricket is a national obsession in Sri Lanka, and the national team's exploits are followed religiously. Test matches are mainly held in Colombo and Galle, and one-day internationals in Colombo, Galle, Kandy, Dambulla and Hambantota. Cricketing specialists Red Dot Tours (www.reddottours.com) are the go-to option for arranging cricket tours, whether as a spectator or participant

Diving and watersports

There are excellent PADI-licensed dive centres all over the island, and diving packages and courses are good value compared to many other places in the world. Hikkaduwa is the main diving centre on the west coast, while over on the east coast there are a number of reputable outfits in Uppuveli and Nilveli, not to mention at least a dozen other operators scattered around the coast.

Bentota is the island's main watersports centre, with various places offering windsurfing, jet-skiing, tubing, water-skiing and more, while on the west coast, Kalpitiya has established an international reputation as one of the world's best kitesurfing centres, with dozens of kite camps now established across the area. The island's best snorkelling is at Pigeon Island, near Trincomalee on the east coast, while Kitulgala in the hill country is where you'll find the island finest whitewater rafting on the choppy waters of the Kelani Ganga.

Surfing

Sri Lanka's surfing scene has taken off big time over the past decade, offering a wide range of waves and breaks to suit all abilities. The stand-out destination is Arugam Bay on the east coast, the one place in Sri Lanka with an international surfing reputation. There are also great surf spots all along the south coast, including Hiriketiya, Weligama, Midigama/Ahangama, Medawatta (at SK Town Beach) and Madiha. On the west coast, Hikkaduwa is the leading surf venue, and there are also passable if not outstanding waves at the popular resorts of Unawatuna and Mirissa. Boards for hire and surfing tuition are available at all these places. The surfing season runs from April to October at Arugam Bay, and from November to April along the south and west coasts.

Cricket is massively popular

Whale- and dolphin-watching

Sri Lanka has emerged since the late noughties as one of Asia's leading whale-watching destinations, with regular sighting of blue whales and other cetacean species (and often dolphins as well). Mirissa on the south coast is the main centre, with half a dozen local operators running tours, while trips also run from Uppuveli on the east coast. The best times are December and April on the south coast, and March/April and August/September on the east.

Ballooning

There are currently two balloon operators in Sri Lanka, Lanka Balloon (www.srilankaballoon.com) and Sun Rise Ballooning (www.srilanka ballooning.com), both offering daily flights (weather permitting) from November to April, taking off from the *Kandalama Hotel* near Dambulla and offering bird's-eye views of local forests and plains. Flights last about an hour and cost around $200 per person.

Walking

The island's hill country (see tours 5 and 6) is a walker's paradise, with stunning scenery and a pleasant temperate climate. Many of the islands major tour operators can organise walking trips. Alternatively contact local guides such as Sumane Bandara Illangantilake (www.trekkingexpeditor.com) or Ravi Desappriya (www.srilankatrekking.com), both in Kandy. Also worth checking out is the new Pekoe Trail (www.thepekoetrailsrilanka.com), Sri Lanka's first long-distance footpath.

Ayurveda, spas and yoga

The traditional system of holistic health care known as Ayurveda (from the Sanskrit, meaning 'the science of life') has been practised in India and Sri Lanka for centuries. According to the Ayurvedic system, all bodies are made up of varying combinations of the five basic elements (ether, fire, air, earth and water) and governed by three *doshas* (*pitta*, *vata* and *kapha*). Rather than treating illnesses and symptoms in isolation, Ayurveda aims to treat the whole patient in order to encourage a more balanced lifestyle. Resorts island-wide provide Ayurveda therapies ranging from long-term residential retreats through to one-off spa-style treatments.

There are also lots of quality spas at hotels around the island, usually offering Ayurveda-style therapies alongside classic international spa treatments. Yoga is also increasingly popular, particularly along the south coast, where there are now dozens of guesthouses offering yoga programmes, often sold in combination with surfing packages.

An Ayurvedic soak

Diving in the Indian Ocean

Chronology

Sri Lanka's history has frequently been a violent one – though thankfully its most recent major conflict, the civil war between the Liberation Tigers of Tamil Eelam (LTTE) and the Sri Lanka military, finally ended in 2009.

Early history

543 BC Death of the Buddha in India and the arrival of Prince Vijaya from India with 700 followers to become the island's first king.
380 BC The island's first capital is established at Anuradhapura.
c.250–210 BC Reign of Devanampiya Tissa. The king and population convert to Buddhism.
205 BC The Indian warrior Elara captures Anuradhapura.
161–137 BC Elara is defeated by Dutugemunu; Sri Lanka is unified under a single Sinhalese monarch for the first time.
AD 993 The Cholas of South India capture Anuradhapura and the capital is moved to Polonnaruwa.

Colonial period

1505 The Portuguese arrive and extract concessions from the king of Kotte.
1656 The Dutch oust the Portuguese from the island and introduce Dutch law.
1796 The Dutch surrender the island to the British during the Napoleonic Wars.
1815 The last Sri Lankan king is captured at Kandy by the British, ending 24 centuries of Sinhalese monarchy. For the first time, the whole island falls under foreign rule.
1820s New roads open up the interior of the island to British settlers.
1867 Tea is introduced to Sri Lanka following the collapse of the coffee industry; the island's first railway line, from Colombo to Kandy, enters service.
1931 Universal franchise is granted.

Independence

1948 Ceylon is granted independence.
1959 Prime Minister S.W.R.D. Bandaranaike assassinated by a Buddhist monk.
1960 His widow, Sirimavo Bandaranaike, becomes world's first woman prime minister.
1971 Armed rebellion by Maoist JVP in south leaves thousands dead.
1972 The country's colonial name, Ceylon, is changed to Sri Lanka.
1978 A new constitution introduces the office of executive president, with J.R. Jayewardene as the first president.

A kolam drama production, 1878

Ethnic strife

1983 'Black July' sees the LTTE attack on the army in the north sparking ethnic clashes. Thousands of Tamil civilians in Colombo are murdered by Sinhalese mobs, leading to the outbreak of civil war.
1987–8 A second JVP insurrection. Thousands more die in the south.
1993 President Premadasa is assassinated by the LTTE.
1994 Chandrika Bandaranaike Kumaratunga is elected president while her mother, Sirimavo Bandaranaike, is prime minister.
1996 Sri Lanka's cricket team wins the World Cup.
2004 The devastating South Asian tsunami kills more than 30,000 and leaves 100,000 homeless.
2006 Mahinda Rajapakse becomes president.
2007 The Sri Lankan army succeeds in driving the LTTE out of eastern Sri Lanka.
2009 The Sri Lankan army, led by General Sarath Fonseka, defeats the LTTE. Tiger leader Prabakaran is killed and all rebel-held territory reclaimed.
2010 Mahinda Rajapakse re-elected (his main opponent, General Sarath Fonseka, is arrested on conspiracy charges).
2015 Maithripala Sirisena defeats Rajapakse and becomes president.
2019 Attacks by Islamist terror group National Thowheeth Jama'ath in Colombo, Negombo and Batticaloa kill around 269 people.
2020 Mahinda Rajapakse's brother and former defence chief Gotabaya Rajapakse elected president.
2021–22 Deepening economic crisis, exacerbated by Covid, grips Sri Lanka. Essential supplies run dangerously low and government declares country bankrupt. Gotabaya resigns amidst widespread popular protests and is replaced by Ranil Wickremesinghe.
2024 Economy slowly recovering under package of emergency austerity measures.

President Ranil Wickremesinghe

A tsunami memorial at Kalutara

TRIP PLANS

WALK 1
Colombo Fort and Pettah

A walk through the heart of old Colombo, starting with a walk around the grandiose colonial buildings of Fort district before continuing on to the bustling Pettah shopping district.

DISTANCE: 4km (2.5 miles)
TIME: Half a day
START: Presidential Secretariat
END: World Trade Centre
POINTS TO NOTE: This walk starts and ends in the High Security Zone – avoid taking photographs of soldiers, police checkpoints or anything else that might be considered sensitive from a security point of view.

Colombo, Sri Lanka's colonial heart, is a fascinating reflection of the island's contrasts: from the rifle-toting soldiers defending the High Security Zone in central Fort to cheery shopkeepers and street hawkers in Pettah's crowded markets; and from decaying colonial office blocks to the brash modern glass-fronted towers of the World Trade Centre and surrounding high-rises.

Fort

Fort district was formerly the administrative and financial heart of the city, occupied for 450 years by the Portuguese, Dutch and British in turn – some old cannons remain by the Presidential Secretariat, although there is no trace of the old fort ramparts. Repeated LTTE attacks during the civil war – including a devastating bomb blast outside the Central Bank in 1996 – largely killed off the commercial life of the area, and although the area has revived significantly since, parts of the area remain out of bounds thanks to the presence of the President's House.

The Presidential Secretariat

Start at the **Presidential Secretariat** ❶ building (formerly the parliament) overlooking the northern end of Galle Face Green, with its neoclassical columns, steep steps and statues of independent Sri Lanka's first four prime ministers standing in front.

From the roundabout in front of the Secretariat, the seafront promenade runs alongside the Kingsbury hotel to reach the city's **lighthouse** (1951), from where you can look out over the vast swathe of reclaimed land currently being developed as the new Port City project. Beyond the

Colombo's skyline in the evening

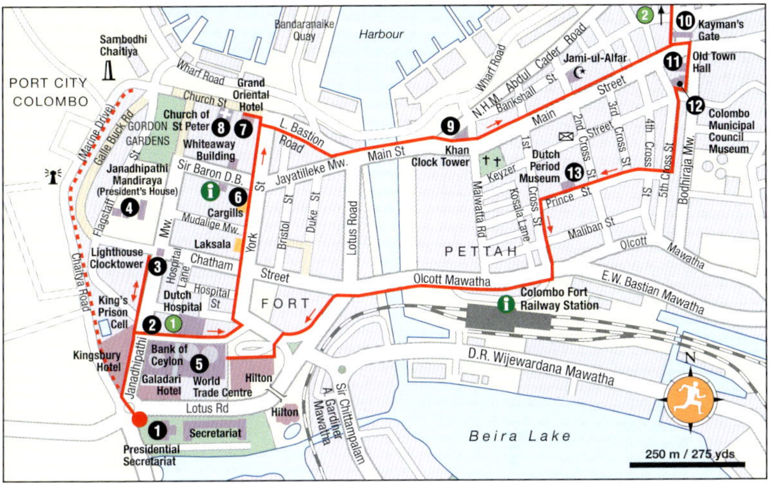

lighthouse is the quirky **Sambodhi Chaitiya**, a towering Buddhist stupa-on-stilts dating from 1956.

King's Prison Cell

Return to the roundabout opposite the Secretariat and walk up Janadhipathi Mawatha. At the first junction (in the car park of the Fort Police Station) look out for the small domed **cell** ❷ where Sri Wickrama Rajasinghe, the last king of Kandy (from 1798 to 1815), is said to have been imprisoned by the British after the conquest of Kandy.

Continue up Janadhipathi Mawatha to reach the city's quaint old **lighthouse clocktower** ❸, originally built in 1857 to serve both as a beacon for local shipping and a useful timepiece for watchless locals. This is as far as you can currently walk. Beyond the security barriers (but largely obscured by trees) is the **President's House** ❹, built by the last Dutch governor in the eighteenth century.

Retrace your steps then turn east and along Bank of Ceylon Mawathatha to reach the soaring Bank of Ceylon headquarters and the twin towers of the **World Trade Centre** ❺, Colombo's tallest buildings. Directly opposite, the beautifully restored seventeenth-century **Dutch Hospital** is now home to an excellent little cluster of cafes, restaurants and shops including the excellent **Ceylon Curry Club** restaurant, see ①.

Tuk-tuks ply Colombo's streets

Colonial buildings

Head to York Street, and then turn north past the government-run **Laksala** handicrafts emporium (60 York Street). A few steps further north is the vast puce-red bulk of **Cargills** ❻ (40 York Street), Colombo's oldest department store, established in 1844. Plaster horns of plenty adorn the rooftop, although the interior is now almost completely empty save a mini-market and a deeply incongruous branch of KFC. Just north of here on Sir Baron Jayatilaka Mawatha, the beautifully restored, vaguely French-looking building of 1907 originally housed the **Whiteaway, Laidlaw & Co.** department store, nicknamed "Right away and paid for", since no goods were sold on credit.

Another of Fort's graceful (although now rather dilapidated) old colonial buildings, the **Grand Oriental Hotel** ❼, sits at the end of York Street. Originally built as an army barracks in 1837, the Grand Oriental was subsequently turned into a hotel in 1875. Next door in Church Street, behind a police barricade, is the hauntingly time-warped **St Peter's Church** ❽, originally the reception of the Dutch governor's residence.

Pettah

Walk east past a series of mildewed colonial buildings along Leyden Bastion Road and cross the small canal linking the harbour with **Beira Lake** to reach **Khan Clock Tower** ❾, erected in 1923.

Beyond Khan Clock Tower you enter **Pettah**, Colombo's helter-skelter bazaar area, usually thronged with dense crowds of shoppers, hawkers and porters jostling amidst the crowded streets. The name comes from the Tamil word *pettai* (old town). This was once a prime residential area but degenerated into 'the native quarter' as the British colonists moved out to build homes in the suburbs. Each of the side roads leading south off Main Street specialises in a different type of goods – electronics, fabrics, spices and so on – with colourful shops stuffed full of every conceivable type of merchandise, ranging from cut-price mobile phones to cheap saris.

Municipal mementoes

At the far end of Main Street is **Kayman's Gate** ❿, although all that remains of the original gateway is a belfry, dating from the Dutch period. The gate is allegedly named after the caimans (crocodiles) which once infested the local waterways, either (depending on who you believe) attracted to the city by food scraps or put there deliberately by the Dutch to deter slaves from escaping by swimming to freedom. If you're ready for a bite in air-conditioned surroundings, head a short ways

The Cargills building

north up Sea Street, for a bargain lunch at **Sri Suryas**, see ❸.

Facing Kayman's Gate from the south side of the junction is the striking **Old Town Hall** ⓫ of 1873, adorned with minaret-like towers and retaining the double portico that once gave access to horse-drawn carriages. An open-sided wrought-iron pavilion next door houses the **Colombo Municipal Council Museum** ⓬ (free), home to a weird array of colonial-era industrial and municipal hardware including a steamroller, old street signs and a former van of the Colombo Public Library.

Dutch Period Museum

Head south down 5th Cross Street then turn west into Prince Street, crowded with shops selling glass and mirrors. Towards the western end of the street the old Dutch town hall of 1780 is now home to the **Dutch Period Museum** ⓭, filled with colonial furniture and household items. The museum has been closed for renovations for years now and with no reopening date so far announced, although the elegantly collonaded colonial façade, incongruously squashed in amongst brash modern shops, is well worth a look.

Leaving the museum, turn south down 1st Cross Street to emerge in the frenzy of Olcott Mawatha in front of **Fort Railway Station**, the country's main rail terminal. The road is named after the famous American Buddhist missionary Henry Steel Olcott (1832–1907), whose statue stands in front of the station. Olcott spent many years in Sri Lanka and also helped design the distinctive Buddhist flag which now flutters above temples around the island, and indeed worldwide.

Food and drink

❶ Ceylon Curry Club

Dutch Hospital; www.ceyloncurryclub.com; $$$

The classic flavours of traditional Sri Lankan cuisine are given an inventive contemporary twist at this good-looking restaurant – sweet potato roti with jackfruit puree, curried brinjal (aubergine) ravioli and even a Ceylon-style beef Wellington, to name just three – all beautifully prepared and artfully presented.

❸ Sri Suryas

255 Sea Street; $

A great spot for lunch while exploring Pettah, this pleasant a/c restaurant serves up excellent subcontinental chow at bargain prices, majoring in South Indian thalis and dosas but with a good selection of North Indian classics too.

Crowded Pettah streets

TOUR 2
Modern Colombo

Hire a tuk-tuk or taxi for this enjoyable tour of modern Colombo's eclectic sights, including the city's most flamboyant Buddhist temple, its grandest park and a couple of modern monuments, rounded off with a visit to the excellent National Museum and some shopping on Galle Road.

DISTANCE: 25km (15.5 miles)
TIME: Half a day
START: Gangaramaya Temple
END: Galle Face Hotel
POINTS TO NOTE: You could hire a hotel taxi to do this tour but it's cheaper and more fun to pick up a three-wheeler rickshaw (tuk-tuk) to get between the various sights. Tuk-tuk fares should always be agreed before setting off – ask at your hotel first to get an idea of what to pay, and then bargain like crazy. And if you can't get the fare you want just walk away – you'll have plenty more offers. Taxis and tuk-tuks will wait while you sightsee or shop. A tip of about five percent of the fare for a hotel taxi should be sufficient.

From Fort, Colombo stretches south down the west coast to the commercial suburbs of Kollupitiya and Bambalapitiya, and bulges eastwards inland to Slave Island, mixing swanky modern developments with raffish old-school charm. Past here are the broad avenues of upmarket Cinnamon Gardens, home to the city's excellent National Museum.

Slave Island

Start the day by catching a tuk-tuk (or taxi) to the sprawling **Gangaramaya Temple** ❶ (www.gangaramaya.com; charge), at the southern edge of the area known as **Slave Island** on account of the captives formerly kept here by the Portuguese. Colombo's most impressive shrine, the Gangaramaya is packed with a picturesque medley of shrines, statues and stupas arranged a diminutive courtyard shaded by a huge bo tree. The temple also houses a bizarre **museum** showcasing items presented by devotees featuring an eclectic range of items from vintage motorcars to what is claimed to be the world's smallest Buddha state, so tiny that a magnifying glass is provided to see it in detail.

A bridge over Beira Lake

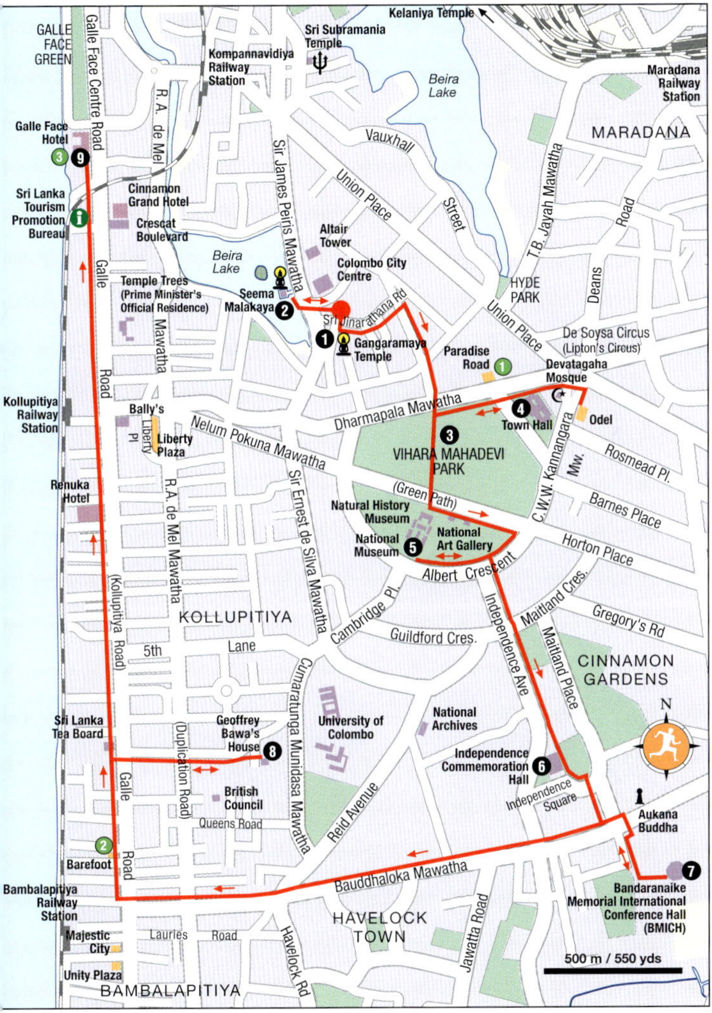

At Gangaramaya Temple

Seema Malaka and Beira Lake

It's a couple of minutes' walk from here to the **Seema Malakaya** ❷ (included in Gangaramaya Temple ticket), designed by the great Sri Lankan architect Geoffrey Bawa (1919–2003). Used for religious ceremonies by monks from the nearby Gangaramaya Temple, this is one of the prettiest sights in central Colombo, with three linked pavilions set amidst the serene waters of Beira Lake, connected to the shore by a narrow wooden bridge.

You're now at the southwestern end of **Beira Lake** – not actually a lake in the conventional sense but a system of man-made waterways looping around Slave Island, first created by the Portuguese to provide protection against attackers, and variously expanded and modified by the Dutch and British (the name is either from the Portuguese 'Beira' or the Dutch 'De Beer'). The waters here are particularly pretty, with a small island (accessible by footbridge) out in the middle and lots of aquatic birdlife including pelicans, herons, cormorants and storks.

Immediately behind the Seema Malaka on the waterfront rise the colourful new **Colombo City Centre** mall and the distinctly sloping **Altair Tower** – two of the various ambitious developments which are now transforming this area of the city beyond recognition.

Cinnamon Gardens

Return to the Gangaramaya Temple then continue northeast along Sri Jinarathana Rd to reach the junction with Park Street, with a vast banyan temple filling the central roundabout. Head south down Park Street, passing Park Street Mews (home to an excellent little cluster of restaurants) and then cross busy Dharmapala Mawatha to reach **Vihara Mahadevi Park** ❸. The city's most attractive park, this is all that remains of what was once a vast plantation of cinnamon trees lying at the western edge of the upmarket suburb still known as **Cinnamon Gardens**, dotted with stately old villas.

On the north side of the park, the impressive **Town Hall** ❹ resembles a miniature version of the Capitol building in Washington, DC, while directly behind rise the spiky miniature minarets of the eye-catching **Devatagaha Mosque**. Directly opposite, the **Odel** shopping complex (www.odel.lk) is one of the city's best and busiest shopping destinations and a great place to pick up local clothing labels, souvenirs and books. There are also several eating outlets here, although it's nicer to head over the road to the more peaceful café at the **Paradise Road** boutique, see ❶, an Aladdin's cave of contemporary homeware, crafts and souvenirs.

The National Museum

Head back south across Viharamahadevi

Statuary in the National Museum

Park to **Green Path** – you might see some paintings for sale by local artists hung up on the railing here, particularly if you visit at the weekend, when the entire road transforms into an impromptu open-air gallery. Walk east down the road, past the striking modern Nelum Pokuna Theatre, with its lotus-inspired design, then back down Albert Crescent to reach the impressive **Colombo National Museum** ❺ (charge). Housed in a grand colonial building of 1877, the museum's extensive collection ranges from Buddhist statues and royal regalia to kitchen utensils and antique puppets.

Independence Avenue

Retrace your steps east along Albert Crescent then head south down Independence Avenue to reach the **Independence Commemoration Hall** ❻, built shortly after Sri Lanka gained independence from Britain in 1948. It's actually a copy of the Audience Hall at The Temple of the Tooth, although built in stone rather than wood. Cricket enthusiasts might want to make the short detour east to the venerable **Sinhalese Sport Club**, the island's principal test-match venue.

Immediately south of here lies the Independence Arcade complex, a cool white colonial landmark of 1882 occupying the former Colombo Asylum. The complex is spread over two buildings: the Entrance Wing, with cute little cupola and clock, and the H-shaped Main Wing, both now home to an upmarket array of restaurants, cafés and boutiques.

Diagonally opposite, the octagonal **Bandaranaike Memorial International Conference Hall** ❼ (BMICH) on Bauddhaloka Mawatha was a gift from the Chinese government in memory of Sri Lanka's assassinated prime minister S.W.R.D. Bandaranaike (1899–1959). A replica of the famous **Aukana Buddha statue** stands outside.

Galle Road

Catch a tuk-tuk from here for the short ride west to Galle Road, southern Colombo's major highway which arrows due south along the coast. Stop for a late lunch at the beautiful **Barefoot** café, see ②, occupying an idyllic courtyard at the back of Colombo's best-loved shop. A city institution, Barefoot is famous for its colourful handloom fabrics, and also hosts regular exhibitions in the attached gallery as well as regular jazz afternoons and other events.

Geoffrey Bawa's House

After lunch, it's just a short walk across Galle Road and then up Alfred House Road to the beautiful **Gallery Café**, located in the former offices of celebrated Sri Lankan architect Geoffrey Bawa, now home to a gorgeous courtyard restaurant and small shop.

Gangaramaya temple ceiling

Crowds outside the BMICH

Food and drink

❶ Paradise Road Café
213 Dharmapala Mawatha; www.paradiseroad.lk; $$
Set on the tiny balcony of the Paradise Road emporium and serving good coffee and delicious cakes, along with a short menu of light meals and daily specials.

❷ Barefoot Café
704 Galle Road; www.barefootceylon.com; $$
Soothing courtyard café serving a tempting selection of tasty light meals (including excellent daily specials), snacks, salads and cakes.

❸ The Traveller's Bar
Galle Face Hotel, 2 Galle Road; www.gallefacehotel.com; $$$
Upmarket colonial-style bar in the city's most historic hotel, plastered with a photo gallery of the many famous people who have stayed here. Or head to the hotel's contemporary chill-out Firebeach lounge for sunset cocktails.

Continue up Duplication Road (officially R.A. de Mel Mawatha) then turn right onto Bagatelle Road and then right again down tiny 33rd Lane to reach **Geoffrey Bawa's House** ❽ (no.11, 33rd Lane; charge), being sure to time your visit to coincide with the afternoon tour of the property (see www.geoffreybawa.com for details). One of Colombo's buried treasures and a real unique experience, this distinctive house comprises what were originally four tiny bungalows, which Bawa acquired between 1959 and 1968 and then set about dramatically remodelling, knocking the four buildings together and constructing a magical little labyrinth of rooms, courtyards, lightwells, verandas and passageways.

Galle Face Green

Catch a tuk-tuk back to Galle Face Green and end your day with a sundowner at the beautiful **Traveller's Bar**, see ❸, in Colombo's oldest and most famous hotel, the venerable **Galle Face Hotel** ❾ (established 1864).

As the sun sets, stroll north across the breezy oceanfront expanse of **Galle Face Green**, Colombo's best-loved public space – the whole place comes alive at sunset and early evening, when half the city seems to come here to gossip, fly kites and eat the crunchy *isso wade* (prawn patties) served up by the line of hawkers stretched out along the front. Make the enjoyable twenty-minute wander back to Fort and then settle in for dinner at the excellent **Curry Club** (see page 33).

The National Museum's imposing exterior

TOUR 3
Negombo via the Wetlands

Head north through the sprawling suburbs of Colombo to the untamed wetland wilderness of Muthurajawela, an area of unspoilt nature close to the ever-expanding capital, before continuing on to the lively beach resort of Negombo.

DISTANCE: 40km (25 miles)
TIME: A leisurely day
START: Colombo
END: Negombo
POINTS TO NOTE: This is a good tour with which to begin or end a visit to Sri Lanka, offering a rare insight into the island's lagoon and mangrove-fringed coastline as well as the chance to enjoy the restaurants and bars of Negombo – one of the island's livelier beach resorts, just a twenty-minute drive from the airport. Note that although the route starts in Colombo, it can be done just as easily as a round-trip from Negombo itself.

One of the largest towns along the west coast, Negombo rose to prominence during the colonial era thanks to its abundant supplies of wild cinnamon. The centre of town preserves a few reminders of the Dutch period, including the remains of an old fort (converted by the British into a prison and still used as such), a ramshackle old rest house, and the Dutch canal, which heads north from Negombo to Puttalam, over 100km (62 miles) away.

Muthurajawela

Leave Colombo by 6am at the latest if you want to take the first boat tour of the day (at 7am) and see marsh bird life at its best at the **Muthurajawela Wetlands**. The first boat leaves daily at 7am, with trips continuing throughout the day until 4pm. Whenever you arrive, it's a good idea to call in advance to ensure that there's a boat available.

Driving out of Colombo on the A3 (the old coastal highway), it seems incredible that an ecological haven could be found anywhere near the highway's traffic and factory yards. To reach the wetlands, turn off the A3 at the busy suburb of **Ja-Ela**, heading left down Bopitiya Road for 3km (2 miles) to reach the wetlands.

Wetlands

Arriving at the **Muthurajawela Wetlands** ❶ (charge) you'll see the

Brightly coloured post boxes in Negombo

compound of thatched huts housing the visitor centre where knowledgeable guides will give you a quick introduction to the reserve's ecology before ushering you into an open boat.

The saltwater wetlands are home to abundant bird life as well as to toque macaque monkeys, water monitors and the occasional crocodile. The boat putters down the Hamilton Canal before reaching the southern end of the **Negombo Lagoon**, a breezy expanse of water running around patches of tangled mangrove swamp with egrets, herons and kingfishers perched in the branches.

Negombo

Return to the A3 and head north past the turn-off to the Colombo

Cinnamon

One of Sri Lanka's most attractive commodities, in the eyes of the Dutch, was the plentiful cinnamon that grew wild in the island's jungles. Cinnamon was in huge demand in Europe, where it was valued for its flavour and as an aid to digestion. Cinnamon found in the Negombo area was regarded as the sweetest, and hence the most highly prized. Cinnamon was so valuable that it was made a capital offence to trade it illegally. However, Arab traders were more familiar than Dutch naval patrols with the Negombo coast, so smuggling cinnamon was a lucrative endeavour.

International Airport. Continue down a wide dual carriageway and after 5km (3 miles), turn west at the Ceypetco petrol station down Archbishop Nicholas Marcus Fernando Mawatha to **Negombo** ❷. The railway line is on one side and shops are on the other as you head into the busy town.

Bounding the south side of the old town centre, the Negombo Lagoon is the source of some of the island's most highly prized seafood, especially its large

Fishing boats in Negombo harbour

and juicy prawns. Daily fish auctions are held early in the morning (around 7am) in the busy fish markets in the town centre and at Duwa, both worth a visit for the sight of crowds of locals haggling animatedly over huge piles of tuna, seer, mullet, crabs and more.

St Mary's Church

In the middle of town stands the stately white landmark of **St Mary's Church**, one of the many large Roman Catholic churches that dot Negombo. Portuguese missionaries were particularly active in the area, converting many of the local Karava fishermen. Their devotion to Roman Catholicism can still be seen, not only in the churches but also in the dozens of beautiful little wayside shrines.

From the church it's worth taking a quick turn around the old town centre, heading south down St Mary's Street to reach the lagoon, with hundreds of multicoloured fibreglass boats tied up, and then looping anticlockwise past the old Dutch Fort, the main fish market, and back down Main Street, lined with pretty colonial-era houses.

From here, Sea Street runs north for 1.5km, parallel to the sea, before reaching the junction with Lewis Place. Turn left into Lewis Place and continue along the road, dotted with innumerable guesthouses and travellers' cafés, to reach Porutota Road in the suburb of **Ettukala**, the main beach and hotel area, Here try **Lords**, see 1, or **Tuk Tuk Wine and Dine**, see 2, for some refreshments.

Food and drink

1 Lords
80B Porutota Road;
www.lordsrestaurant.net; $$$
Attractive modern café-cum-restaurant serving up tasty and beautifully presented cuisine from around the world, although Asian flavours predominate, plus a great vegetarian and vegan selection.

2 Tuk Tuk Wine and Dine
52 St Joseph Mawatha;
www.tuktuknegombo.com; $$$
This funky garden restaurant has significantly raised the bar for local nightlife, with cool decor, a great menu of Sri Lankan and international dishes (including a good pizza selection) and regular live music.

Negombo Beach

After leaving your vehicle in Porutota Road, it's a pleasant stroll along the main drag. The beach itself remains largely the preserve of local fishermen mending their nets, making reed baskets or working on their vessels. The sight of the fishing fleet returning to shore in the early morning, in a flotilla of distinctive *oruwa* boats with their huge brown sails, is one of the west coast's most memorable sights. For a trip out to sea, charter an *oruwa* with local boatmen on the beach or through your accommodation.

Negombo Beach is very popular with local families

TOUR 4
Road to Kandy

Visit the world's only elephant orphanage, explore one of Asia's most beautiful botanical gardens, and then drive up to the former royal capital of Kandy to pay your respects at the revered Temple of the Tooth.

DISTANCE: 116km (72 miles)
TIME: Two days
START: Colombo
END: Kandy
POINTS TO NOTE: The following itinerary starts in Colombo but can also be done just as easily from Negombo. Allow two days: one to drive up and one to explore Kandy. This trip can precede tour 5 to Nuwara Eliya and the hill country, or tours 7 and 8 to Anuradhapura and Polonnaruwa, from where you could continue to the east coast beaches.

The road between Colombo and Kandy encapsulates the island's dramatic contrasts: from the flat, sun-drenched coast to the cool heights of the rugged central hill country. En route the journey traverses a fascinating cross-section of Sri Lankan history and culture, including the colonial-era Peradeniya Botanical Gardens, the famous Pinnawala Elephant Orphanage and historic Kandy itself, home to the island's most venerated Buddhist temple.

The original road to Kandy was built in the 1820s. Now, as the A1, it's one of Sri Lanka's busiest modern highways – heavy traffic means the drive from Colombo to Kandy can take anything up to four hours, even before you've factored in time spent exploring sights along the way.

Henerathgoda Botanical Gardens

Check out of your Colombo hotel after breakfast and head out of the capital, taking the Kandy Road at the Kelani Bridge. Some 25km (15.5 miles) from Colombo, stalls in the village of Belummahara line the roadside, selling the sweetest pineapples in the country. Buy them whole, or in pieces sprinkled with chilli powder as a spicy snack.

Turn off the Kandy Road at the 27km (17-mile) marker at **Miriswatta** to make a detour for 6km (4 miles) down the B288 road signposted to **Gampaha**. This leads through paddy fields to the **Henerathgoda Botanical Gardens** (www.bit.ly/henerathgoda; charge) at Asgiriya. Established in 1876, this pretty park contains 400 species of

Inside the Temple of the Tooth

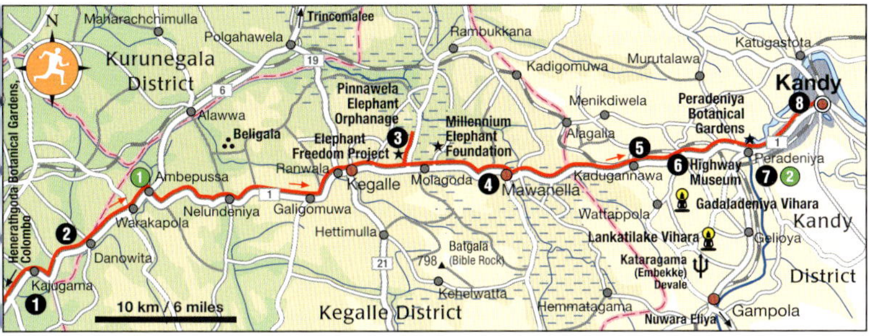

plants in 14.4 hectares (36 acres). You'll probably have the gardens to yourself as they are little visited by tourists.

Kajugama

Return to the A1 at the village of **Yakkala.** North of here, the road is lined with an interesting string of villages, each specialising in a difference craft or produce. These start with Nittambuwa (rambutans), which is also home to the country mansion of the famous Bandaranaike family, who have provided Sri Lanka with no less than three prime ministers.

Next is **Kajugama** ❶, where women stand by the roadside selling cashew nuts *(cadju)* to passing motorists, followed by the cane-weaving village of **Radawadunna** ❷, where craftsmen skilfully weave cane into chairs, baskets and souvenirs. At **Ambepussa**, 60km (37 miles) from Colombo you'll find the country's oldest hotel, the venerable **Ambepussa Rest House** (now the Heritage Ambepussa), see ①, opened in 1828 when the road was being built and a good place for a drink, snack or light meal.

Elephant Orphanages

Continue on the A1 to bustling **Kegalle,** 79km (49 miles) from Colombo, then detour north to reach the **Pinnawala Elephant Orphanage** ❸ (charge). There are around eighty elephants here, best seen during the daily feeding sessions at 9am and 12.15pm, or during twice-daily bathing times (10am–noon and 2–4pm), when the elephants are led down to the shallow waters of the nearby Ma Oya river. Several restaurants overlooking the water offer prime riverside seats from which to watch the elephants lumbering about in the shallows below.

Note that regular allegations of animal cruelty have dogged the orphanage in recent years, and although improvements have been made, it remains a controversial attraction. Alternatives to Pinnawala include

Pinnawala Elephant Orphanage

the nearby Millennium Elephant Foundation (www.millenniumelephantfoundation.com – although that too has received criticism) and the more ethical Elephant Freedom Project (www.elephantfreedomproject.com).

The area around Pinnawala is also dotted with dozens of lush 'spice gardens', all offering free tours during which you can see the island's abundant local produce growing in situ – although guides will also pressure you into buying packets of overpriced cinnamon, cloves, cardamom and so on at the end of your visit.

Bible Rock

Returning to the Kandy Road, the left-hand side of the highway is dominated by the solitary, steep-sided mountain of **Utuwankanda**. At **Mawanella** ❹ look up to see fruit bats hanging from trees along the banks of the Maha Oya (river). As the road climbs up towards Kadugannawa Pass the scenery becomes increasingly breathtaking, with endless miles of huge, craggy green hills, including striking, flat-topped **Bible Rock** (Batgala), named by pious Victorians after its alleged resemblance to a church lectern. Beside the road, stalls sell avocado pears and pungent-smelling durians.

Kadugannawa and the Highway Museum

Climb to the top of the pass at **Kadugannawa** ❺ where a slender obelisk (1832) records the achievements of Captain W.F. Dawson 'whose science and skill planned and executed this road and other works of public utility'. A further memento of colonial-era road-making skills can be found at the unusual **Highway Museum** ❻ (free), an open-air display of steamrollers and antique road-making equipment laid out along the side of the A1.

Around 8km further along the road, the formidable granite building on the southern side of the road at **Peradeniya** ❼ is the imposing Mlesna **Tea Fortress**, see ②, a good place to break your journey, with a good selection of various Ceylon teas and snacks in its café and shop.

Kandy

Laid out around a picture-perfect lake amidst a ring of towering green hills, the historic city of **Kandy** ❽ was the main seat of royal power in the island for several centuries, and home to the last independent king of Ceylon until his overthrow by the British in 1815.

Temple of the Tooth

Kandy's centrepiece is the famous **Temple of the Tooth** Ⓐ (Sri Dalada Maligawa; www.sridaladamaligawa.lk; charge), home to what is said to be a tooth of the Buddha himself, brought to Sri Lanka in the fourth century from India. The tooth itself is kept carefully locked up in a casket within

Deep in prayer

the temple and shown only to the most important of visitors, although you at least can catch a glimpse of the casket during the thrice-daily temple ceremonies *(pujas)* held at 5.30am, 9.30am and 6.30pm. The lavishly decorated temple complex is a superb showcase of traditional Kandyan arts and architecture, while within the temple grounds you'll find a small museum housing the stuffed remains of the magnificent tusker, Raja, who served for many years as the lead elephant in the magnificent **Esala Perahera** procession, held in honour of the Tooth Relic over ten days in July or August.

Kandyan Arts & Crafts Association

If you're staying the night in Kandy, it's well worth taking in one of the various dancing shows performed every evening around town. Arguably the best is held at the **Kandyan Arts & Crafts Association** ❽ on Sangaraja Mawatha (near the Temple of the Tooth), where an hour-long performance of traditional dancing and drumming begins nightly at 5pm, featuring lots of spectacularly costumed, superbly acrobatic Kandyan dancers accompanied by traditional drummers.

Kandy Lake and around

From the colonial **Queen's Hotel** in the centre of town it's a short but beautiful walk along the balustraded waterfront promenade between the temple park fence and the lake. The imposing

Peradeniya Gardens

About 6.5km (4 miles) southwest of Kandy, the Peradeniya Botanical Gardens (www.bit.ly/Peradeniya; charge) are the island's largest and finest. Enclosed in a loop of the Mahaweli Ganga (river), the lush 60-hectare (147-acre) park, originally part of the royal residence of King Kirti Sri Rajasinha (1747–80), became a botanical garden in 1821. The first tea seedlings were planted here in 1824, nearly fifty years before tea proved its worth as a commercially profitable crop.

The gardens offer a bewildering array of tropical trees and plants, centred on the stately Royal Palm Avenue and (at the southern end of the avenue), the Great Lawn, home to Peradeniya's most majestic sight: a huge Javan fig whose sprawling roots and branches create a remarkable natural pavilion. Look out, too, for the Great Circle, dotted with a sequence of memorial trees planted by assorted international bigwigs ranging from the Prince of Wales (1875) to Joseph Tito (1959), as well as the endless fruit bats which dangle spookily from the trees in the wilder northern section of the gardens during the day, before rousing themselves at dusk and flying off to hunt as darkness falls.

Temple offerings

The Temple of the Tooth

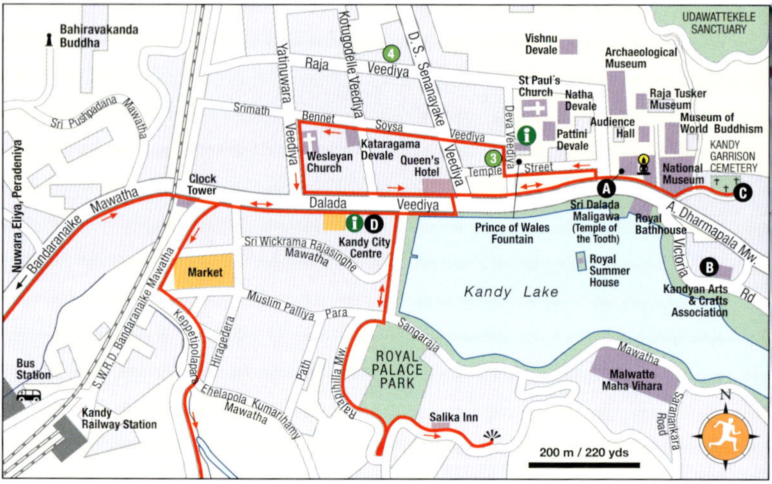

building on the lake's embankment was once the Royal Bathhouse.

At the end of the security fence surrounding the temple, cross the road and walk up the steps opposite. About 100m/yds up the sloping road, a small granite-block lodge marks the entrance to the **Garrison Cemetery** **C** (donation). Here in a neatly-kept setting are the graves of many of the earliest British residents in Kandy, including British diplomat Sir John D'Oyly (1774–1824), who played a crucial role in brokering the surrender of Kandy to British forces in 1815. A perusal of the gravestones reveals the challenging reality of life in the colony, with many dying young of tropical diseases.

Retracing your steps brings you back to the **Kandy National Museum** (www.museum.gov.lk; charge), with a fine array of traditional arts and crafts, while just up the side road from here the quirky **Museum of World Buddhism** (www.ibm.sridaladamaligawa.lk; charge) has entertaining displays on the history of the religion across Asia.

The city centre

Retrace your steps back along the lake towards the centre, then walk in front of the temple entrance and around the other side along Temple Street. Turn northwards past an open-sided Kandyan pavilion to enter Deva Veediya street.

A minute's walk north brings you to the time-warped **St Paul's Church**,

Kandyan dancing

a relic of colonial Anglicanism inserted right in the heart of Sri Lanka's holiest Buddhist district. Immediately south, a gateway leads into the extensive walled compound fronting the Temple of the Tooth which is home to a trio of atmospheric old temples dedicated respectively to Pattini, Natha and Vishnu.

After exploring the temples, return to St Paul's and then head westwards along either Srimath Bennet Soysa Veediya or Dalada Veediya to enter Kandy's main shopping district. Pride of place goes to the swanky modern **Kandy City Centre** D, although elsewhere commercial life continues along more old-fashioned lines, with hundreds of shoebox-sized shops squeezed in along the main roads and surrounding alleyways selling everything from Ayurvedic medicines to mobile phones. For a bite to eat, stop at the bustling the **Empire Café** 3 or the beautiful old **Royal Bar & Hotel**, see 4.

For a magnificent overview of the city, walk up **Rajapihilla Mawatha**, running above the south side of the lake, to the viewpoint at the top, from where you can look down over the whole of Kandy including the Temple of the Tooth, instantly recognisable thanks to the distinctive golden roof which can be seen gleaming above the central shrine. From here, it's worth carrying on to have a drink in the eccentric **Helga's Folly** (see page 92), one of Sri Lanka's zaniest hotels.

Food and drink

1 Ambepussa Rest House

Ambepussa; $$

Marking the halfway point between Colombo and Kandy, this rest house is very popular with local travellers for rice and curry lunches or sandwiches in an old-school atmosphere.

2 Tea Fortress

445 Kandy Road, Peradeniya; $$

Purpose-built emporium, constructed in the form of a rather forbidding-looking granite fortress, selling various grades of tea as well as cakes and snacks.

3 Empire Café

21 Temple Street; $$$

Cute little café in an old colonial building near the Temple of the Tooth serving up a wide range of international dishes – rice and curry, mac and cheese, and assorted burgers, plus good juices and smoothies.

4 Royal Bar & Hotel

44 Raja Vidiya; $$$

Set in what's claimed to be the oldest tavern in Kandy, this gorgeously time-warped venue has bags of olde-world colonial character and superior food, plus a good drinks list.

Tuk-tuks awaiting fares

Scenic Kandy Lake

TOUR 5
Hill Country

This tour through tea-clad hillsides to the former colonial retreat of Nuwara Eliya offers a memorable glimpse of the hill country and provides a welcome respite from the heat of the coast, with a pleasantly temperate (and sometimes positively chilly) climate, despite lying within seven degrees of the Equator.

DISTANCE: 248km (154 miles)
TIME: Two days
START: Kandy
END: Colombo
POINTS TO NOTE: A great alternative to going by road is to take the spectacular hill country railway from Kandy to Nanu Oya (5km from Nuwara Eliya). From Nuwara Eliya, you can then continue on tour 6 to Haputale.

Ringed by green mountains close to the highest part of the island, Nuwara Eliya is one of Sri Lanka's most popular hill resorts, a time capsule of British rule dotted with old colonial-style houses and complete with a breezy boating lake, verdant parks and a picture-perfect golf course. The town was established in 1828 by governor Sir Edward Barnes (1776–1838) who promoted it as a health retreat for British officials wishing to escape the oppressive heat of the lowlands. Barnes' original bungalow was expanded in 1891 to become the mock-Tudor Grand Hotel, setting the style for other buildings and turning Nuwara Eliya into a slice of British nostalgia in the heart of the tropics. Even today Colombo's smart set converge here for Sinhalese New Year in April, when temperatures begin to rise in the capital.

Gampola

Leaving Kandy at the beginning of the morning's drive to Nuwara Eliya, follow the A1 road past the **Peradeniya Botanical Gardens** (see page 45) and then branch off the A1 to pick up the A5 to **Gampola** ❶, 20km (12.5 miles) south of Kandy.

Despite having been the island's capital for a brief spell during the fourteenth century, Gampola's main role nowadays is as the busy gateway town to the hill country's major tea-producing districts. The small **The Heritage Pussellawa** rest house, see ❶, in the village of **Pusselawa** some 20km (12 miles) further along the A5 highway, offers a pleasant stop to break your journey.

Sunset over the tea plantations and Adam's Peak

Ramboda Falls

About 10km (6 miles) past Pusselawa, the road skirts the magnificent **Ramboda Falls** ❷, which tumble over the cliffs in two 100m (328ft) high cascades.

Some 15km (9 miles) before Nuwara Eliya, the **Labookellie Tea Factory** (free) is located in pleasantly cool and breezy countryside around 1,500m (4,921ft) above sea level. The factory hosts guided tours explaining how tea

Tamil tea-pickers at work

is made, as well as offering visitors the chance to walk through the immaculate tea gardens, buy tea to take away or just try a cup in the garden café.

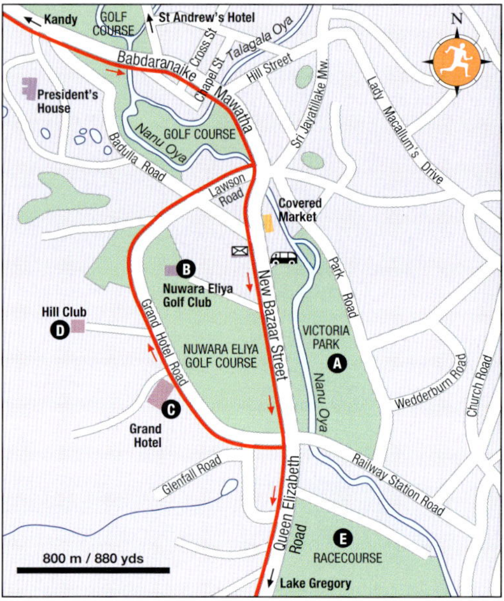

Nuwara Eliya

Another thirty minutes' drive brings you to **Nuwara Eliya** ❸, the highway into town swinging past the stately **St Andrew's Hotel** before reaching New Bazaar Street, the town's main street. This is where you'll find Nuwara Eliya's colourful covered **market**, stacked high with locally grown fruit and vegetables, all selling at much lower prices than in Colombo. Stalls on the opposite side of the road sell woollen sweaters, hats and jackets to help ward off the surprising chill that usually grips Nuwara Eliya at night.

Victoria Park and the golf course

At the southern end of New Bazaar Street a pink brick spire marks the gaudy colonial-built **post office**, while opposite is **Victoria Park** Ⓐ, opened in 1897 and best visited during the April season when it comes alive with blooms. Many of the pioneers who created Nuwara Eliya are buried in the **Anglican Holy Trinity Church** behind the Park.

On the opposite side of the main road through town stretch the beautifully tended links of the **Nuwara Eliya Golf Club** Ⓑ (www.nuwaraeliyagolfclub.com; charge). Established in 1889, this 18-hole course is one of the best, and lushest, in South Asia. Visitors are welcome to play.

Colonial hotels

Tucked away behind the golf course is the sprawling **Grand Hotel** Ⓒ (see page 93), a magnificently old-

Stunning Ramboda Falls

fashioned half-timbered pile which looks like it's been airlifted straight from a golf course in Scotland.

Follow the road as it curves round past the Grand Hotel to reach the similarly incongruous **Hill Club** Ⓓ, a hoary granite hotel steadfastly withstanding modern trends. Its interior, complete with stags' heads and time-worn books, is a perfect period piece, while evening meals – with waiters wearing white gloves – is Sri Lanka's most enduring colonial ritual, seemingly unchanged since the days of empire.

Racecourse and lake

Returning to the main road and heading south brings you to after a further kilometre or so to the town's **racecourse** Ⓔ. The meetings held here in April and August regularly attract Colombo's fashionable set – akin to a Sri Lankan Ascot or Kentucky Derby. Slightly further south is breezy **Lake Gregory**, with boats for hire and a nice waterside path for traffic-free wandering. Standing on the shores of the lake and looking north, you should be able to see (unless it's too misty) the forest-covered heights of **Pidurutalagala** (2,524m, 8,281ft), the highest mountain in Sri Lanka.

For a bird's-eye view out over the surrounding hills, make the pleasant short walk, starting near the racecourse, to **Single Tree Mountain**. Go straight up the road immediately before the Clifton Inn, and walk up through tea plantations to the top, from where (in clear weather) there are marvellous views out to Hakgala and beyond.

Kandapola

One of Sri Lanka's most memorable places to stay – and worth a visit even if you're not overnighting here – the **Heritance Tea Factory Hotel** (see page 93) is located 14km (8.7 miles) from Nuwara Eliya amidst picture-perfect tea plantations around 2,200m (7,214ft) above sea level. The hotel was ingeniously converted from an abandoned tea factory. To reach the hotel, take the road east from the Grand Hotel junction to the plantation town of **Kandapola** ❹, then follow the signs.

Hotel guests can learn to pick their own tea and walk with the hotel's resident naturalist into the wildlife-rich Kuduratte Jungle, while non-guests can still enjoy a walk through the beautiful surrounding tea gardens and a drink or meal inside the ingeniously converted hotel itself or in the memorably quirky **TCK 6685 Restaurant** ❷, located in a converted colonial-era railway carriage.

Hakgala Botanical Gardens

The next day, head 10km (6 miles) south of Nuwara Eliya to the prominent **Hakgala Rock**, whose sheer face rises 450m (1,500ft) above the surrounding countryside. At the foot of the rock lie the pretty **Hakgala Botanical Gardens** ❺ (charge), situated at

Fresh produce for sale

Nuwara Eliya's market

Adam's Peak

Rising south of Hatton is the dramatic mountain of Adam's Peak (2,243 metres; 7,360ft), rising in solitary splendour above the surrounding hills. The Peak has been an object of worship and pilgrimage for centuries amongst the Sinhalese thanks to a strange impression on the bare rock at its summit that is popularly claimed to be a footprint (Sri Pada) made by the Buddha himself during one of his three legendary visits to the island. Thousands of pilgrims haul themselves up the hundreds of steps to the mountain's summit every year to pay their respects to the footprint. The arduous ascent from the village of Dalhousie on the peak's northern side is traditionally made by night during the pilgrimage season from January to April.

just under 2,000m (6,562ft) above sea level and boasting a herbarium, rose garden, fernery and wild orchid collection. The gardens were originally established in 1860 as an experimental plantation of cinchona trees, the source of quinine, the world's leading anti-malarial drug of choice right through until the 1940s and a life-saver in Sri Lanka's early colonial days.

Around 1.5km back up the road to Nuwara Eliya, the modest Hindu **Sita Amman Temple** is said to be built on the spot where Rawana held Sita captive, as related in the great Indian epic the *Ramayana*.

Horton Plains National Park

Beyond Hakgala, at the southern edge of the hill country some 32km (20 miles) from Nuwara Eliya, lies **Horton Plains National Park** ❻ (charge). While the park is home to an interesting array of wildlife including roaming sambhur deer and rare endemic montane bird species, it's the scenery – often shrouded in mist – which is the main attraction. The park offers excellent hikes, the most popular being the 9km (5.5-mile) round trip from the entrance to **World's End**, a stunning viewpoint at the very edge of the hill country where the cliffs fall away for the best part of 1,000m (3,288ft) to the plains below.

From here the trail loops back to the entrance via the quaint **Baker's Falls**, named after Samuel Baker, the famous British explorer who played a key role in the founding of Nuwara Eliya during the 1840s.

Back to Colombo

Returning to the park entrance, you could continue on the A5 to Ella (see page 58) or return to Nuwara Eliya. If you are driving back to Colombo, take the A7 signposted to Hatton through **Nanu Oya** (where you can also catch the train back to Kandy and Colombo). From here, a road leads north off the A7 to **Radella** ❼, where the Somerset

Houses dot the hill country landscape

Food and drink

1 The Heritage Pusselawa
Pusselawa; www.chcplc.com/brands/chc-resthouses/pussellawa; $$
Poised over a magnificent valley view, this provides a reliable lunchtime rice and curry along with other local and international dishes, served in a glass-walled restaurant.

2 TCK 6685 Restaurant
Heritance Tea Factory Hotel, Kandapola; www.heritancehotels.com/teafactory/dining/tck-6685-restaurant.html; $$$
The 'dining room' is actually a gorgeously restored colonial-era railway carriage with lots of polished mahogany, while food features a selection of top-quality Sri Lankan and international options. Open evenings only.

3 Tea Castle
Talawakele; $$
From the outside it looks like a miniature castle, but inside it is a charming restaurant for authentic rice and curry, quality local tea and good cake.

4 Kitulgala Rest House
Kitulgala; tel: 036-228 7528; www.chcplc.com/brands/chc-resthouses/kithulgala; $$
Beautiful old colonial-era dining room overlooking the Kelani Ganga river, with a range of a la carte meals and snacks.

Estate has a shop selling estate-grown tea, plus (in season) strawberries.

Back on the A7 bound for Colombo, drive through glorious tea country to **Talawakele** 8. A few kilometres past Talawakele, two of the hill country's innumerable waterfalls can be seen on the northern side of the road: the broad, step-like St Clair Falls and then, shortly afterwards, the more precipitous Devon Falls. Overlooking the latter, the **Mlesna Tea Castle**, see 3, offers commanding views over the whole valley from its kitsch faux-battlements, and also boasts a handy restaurant and tea shop.

Continuing east along the A7, it's another 15km along the twisty mountain road to the bustling town of **Hatton**, from where you can strike south to **Adam's Peak** (see box), adding a day to your tour if you fancy making the ascent of Sri Lanka's most famous mountain.

Driving east from Hatton it's another 50km (31-mile) to **Kitulgala** 9, now a major white-water rafting centre and also home to an enjoyably time-warped (if now somewhat dilapidated) **Rest House**, see 4, offering a good option for lunch or dinner on the banks of the **Kelani Ganga** river, famous as the location for the shooting of *The Bridge on the River Kwai*. From here, it's another 86km (53 miles) back to Colombo.

Heritance Tea Factory Hotel sign

TOUR 6
Haputale and Ella

This memorable tour traverses some of Sri Lanka's highest and most spectacular scenery, through a landscape of precipitous green hills swathed in endless tea bushes and dotted with a quirky mix of British-era tea bungalows and colourful Hindu temples.

DISTANCE: 70km (43 miles)
TIME: One or two days
START: Nuwara Eliya
END: Ella
POINTS TO NOTE: This journey can also be made by rail from Nanu Oya station (about 5km from Nuwara Eliya) to any one of Haputale, Bandarawela and Ella: this is a memorable two- to three-hour ride along hilltop ridges via the island's highest station, Pattipola, which is located 1,891m (6,203ft) above sea level. From Ella you can drive south for 134km (83 miles) to reach the wildlife haven of Yala National Park (tour 12) or even east to Arugam Bay (tour 11).

This tour starts by heading to Haputale, dramatically perched on the very edge of the hills, before sampling some of the area's old-world colonial charms at Adisham and Bandarawela, and then finishing in the lively tourist hub of Ella.

Nuwara Eliya to Haputale

From Nuwara Eliya, head south along the A5, passing the **Hakgala Botanical Gardens** (see tour 5) along the way. Some 15km (9 miles) beyond the gardens, take the road south at the small town of **Keppetipola which** eventually leads, after innumerable hairpins, to Haputale. En route it's worth stopping by the railway station at **Idalgashina** ❶, located 1,615m (5,298ft) above sea level and offering stunning views of scalloped hills dropping away on both sides of the platform.

Adisham

About 3km (2 miles) before Haputale the country lane brings you to **Adisham** ❷ (open Sat, Sun, *Poya* days and school holidays only, 9.30am–4.30pm; charge). Now used as a monastery and novitiate by the Congregation of St Sylvester, this Gothic-style granite house was originally built in 1931 as the home of Sir Thomas Villiers (1869–1959). His grandfather, Lord John Russell, was twice prime minister of Britain, but Villiers was the

A panoramic view of tea plantations

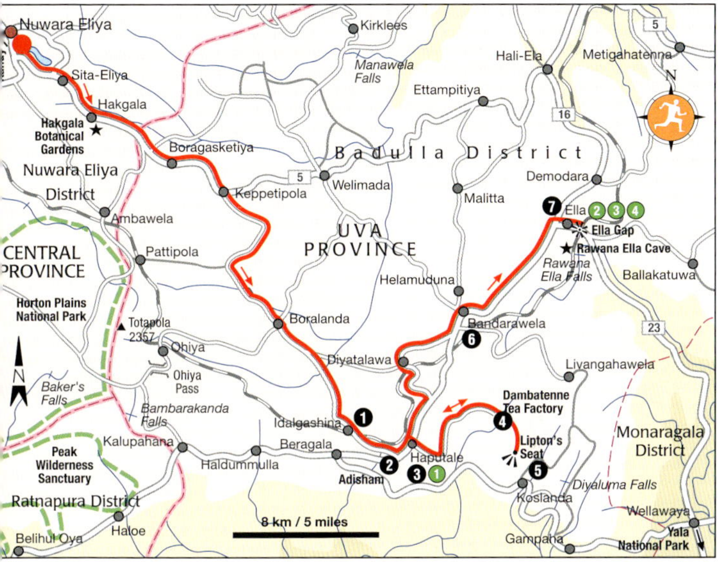

black sheep of the family and arrived in Ceylon in 1887 with ten pounds in his pocket. Villiers subsequently prospered and rewarded himself for his successful business dealings by building Adisham, modelling it on Leeds Castle in Kent and furnishing it with imported carpets, porcelain, furniture and glassware – the fine library remains exactly as Villiers left it.

Spreading away behind Adisham, **Tangamalai Nature Reserve** (open access; free) is also worth a visit, protecting a beautiful area of tropical forest and home to a rich array of bird life, plus a fair few monkeys too.

Haputale

The attraction of **Haputale** ❸ is hard to define. You can walk around the entire town in ten minutes and see where the main road skirts the long drop down to the plains below. But Haputale, in spite of its grubby streets – in strange contrast to the carefully tended tea plantations surrounding it – has an agreeable quality. Perhaps it's the town's compact size, sense of activity, and various eccentricities including a climate that changes from warm sunshine to freezing mist in seconds and the railway track running through the town centre which also

serves as a marketplace for vendors, who have to move their wares quickly whenever a train comes along.

Following the Bandarawela Road east from the centre reveals further sweeping views towards the rolling hills further inland. About ten minutes' walk from town you'll find **St Andrew's**, a simple neo-Gothic barn of a building with a rustic wooden interior – one of the few mementoes of Haputale's colonial past. The churchyard is full of memorials to nineteenth-century tea planters, along with the grave of Reverend Walter Stanley Senior (1876–1938), author of the once-famous *Ode to Lanka*, Victorian Ceylon's great contribution to world literature.

Right in the middle of town by the railway track, local drinking den **High Cliffe**, see ①, offers an offbeat spot for a lunchtime break.

Dambatenne Tea Factory

Beyond Haputale, a narrow road head east for around 5km to reach the **Dambatenne Tea Factory** ❹, one of many estates owned by Sir Thomas Lipton (1848–1931), the Scottish grocer and planter whose novel marketing scheme almost single-handedly put Sri Lankan tea on the global map. Tours of the old-fashioned factory are sometimes available, but get very mixed reviews.

A number of old tea plantation bungalows in the nearby countryside

Kelburne Mountain Resort

also offer memorable stays if you fancy lingering. These include the quaint (and relatively affordable) **Kelburne Mountain View Cottages** and the uber-luxurious **Thotalagala** (www.thotalagala.com), one of the most beautiful plantation bungalows anywhere in Sri Lanka – with prices to match.

Lipton's Seat

Continuing east past Dambatenne the road begins to climb steadily, slaloming between immaculately tended tea gardens and revealing ever-more expansive and sweeping views with each bend – one of the most memorable short drives on the island.

Around 8km past the tea factory you reach the estate's highest point, popularly known as **Lipton's Seat** ❺

Hefting a sack of tea leaves

(charge) after the famous tea magnate, who would often ride his horse up here to survey his plantations. The view from here is one of the finest on the island, looking out from the hill country escarpment, with the lowland plains far below stretching away to the coast – although thick clouds usually roll in by about 10am, so it's best to arrive early if you want to see anything. One enjoyable option if you're staying overnight in Haputale is to catch a taxi or tuk-tuk up to Lipton's Seat first thing and then walk back down again either to Dambatenne or all the way back to Haputale, an easy and immensely enjoyable half-day walk.

Bandarawela

You'll now have to backtrack to Haputale and then pick up the the Bandarawela road (A16), which twists and turns gradually downhill to reach **Bandarawela** ❻. The town itself is bustling and sometimes borderline chaotic, with little to interest casual visitors, although it's worth stopping off for tea at the sedate old **Bandarawela Hotel** (see page 102), built in 1893 when the railway arrived and still boasting an enjoyable tea-planter club atmosphere.

Dowa Cave Temple

Continue northeast along the main Badulla Road (A16). Roughly 6km (4 miles) past Bandarawela, the small **Dowa Cave Temple** stands right by the roadside, although it's easily missed thanks to the thick woodland surrounding it. The main attraction

From leaf to cup

Following the experimental growth of tea by James Taylor at Loolecondra near Kandy (see tour 4) in the 1860s, the topography of highland Sri Lanka was changed for ever. Large tracts of the hill country were cleared by entrepreneurial British settlers, and within 20 years the environment of the hill country was transformed from dense jungle to swathes of neatly manicured tea bushes.

Tea begins its journey from hillside to cup when two top leaves and a bud are gently picked by a tea plucker. The freshly gathered leaves are swiftly transferred to a nearby tea factory where they are withered overnight in blasts of hot air to remove excess moisture. The withered leaves are rolled and crushed by machinery, often dating from Victorian times, to release the remaining sap and to trigger fermentation. The leaves are then fired in enormous ovens before being sifted and graded according to particle size. Orange Pekoe (OP) is the standard size for light tea without milk, while Broken Orange Pekoe Fannings (BOPF) is a smaller-size grade used to make stronger cups of tea mixed with milk and sugar.

Early morning at Ella Gap

A tuk-tuk near Haputale

here is a striking figure carved in bas-relief into the rock above the temple: either the historical Buddha or the future Buddha Maitreya.

Ella

Another 2km (1 mile) down the A16, a turn-off on the right leads to the bustling tourist hub **Ella** 7. Formerly a sleepy village, the whole place has mushroomed prodigiously over the past two decades ago, with the original village now more or less buried under a glut of big new hotels, restaurants, and a prodigious number of guesthouses. It's all far from authentic, but compensates with an excellent selection of places to eat, drink and stay, and even a lively after-dark scene, with plenty of places open until late. Try **Dream Cafe**, see 2, or **Cafe Chill**, see 3.

The main attraction, of course, remains the beautiful surrounding countryside. Ella sits right on the southwestern edge of the hill country, with views down to the plains below through a narrow cleft in the hills, known as **Ella Gap** – one of the island's great views

Little Adam's Peak and Demodara Bridge

There are a number of rewarding walks dot around the village. The most spectacular, and taxing, is the steep 3–4hr climb up and down **Ella Rock**, which towers over the village. Alternatively, a shorter and much less strenuous walk (2–3hr return) leads to the nearby **Little Adam's Peak**, with further memorable views down through Ella Gap and across to Ella Rock opposite. To reach the peak, take the Passara Road north out of the village for around 1km, then look for the signed footpath heading off on the right. The cheery little **Adam's Breeze** café, see 4, by the start of the footpath, is a good place to break the walk.

From here it's possible to extend the walk by continuing down Passara Road and past the Newburgh Tea Factory. About 100m past the factory you'll see three small roads going off to the left. Take the left-hand road and walk downhill for twenty minutes to reach the railway line, then turn left and cross the impressive **Demodara Nine Arch Bridge**. Just past here you can follow the tracks through a short tunnel (about 100m long – a bit gloomy, and with a few bats in the middle) before emerging back into daylight. From here, carry on along the railway track, which will bring you back to Ella station in another 30–40 minutes or so.

Rawana Ella Cave and Falls

Ella is also famous as one of the Sri Lankan sites most closely associated with the Ramayana, and particularly with the villainous Ravana, who is

Flowers blooming at the roadside

Food and drink

1 High Cliffe
15 Station Road, Haputale; $
Attached to one of Haputale's oldest hotels, this quaint little bar-restaurant makes a good spot for lunch, often with an eclectic crowd of locals in attendance and a decent selection of Sri Lankan snacks and mains – try the beef with deep-fried garlic.

2 Dream Café
Main Street, Ella; $$$
One of the best of Ella's ever-growing number of cafés. Standards of cooking are high and cover plenty of culinary bases, ranging from rice and curry through to pasta, burgers, wraps and salads, not to mention the best pizza in the hill country. Also does good breakfasts, both Western and Sri Lankan.

3 Cafe Chill
Main Street; $$$
At the heart of the main drag, this vibrant restaurant is one of the liveliest and latest-opening places in the village, with seating either on the streetside veranda or around the back by the open kitchen – or just have a drink on the rooftop terrace under a spectacular thatched roof. Food comprises a decent spread of local and international fare – the pizza is good, as is the bargain eight-dish rice and curry.

4 Adam's Breeze
Passara Road (just before the 1km post and the path off to Little Adam's Peak); $$
A nice place to stop for a drink or food on the way to or from Little Adam's Peak, with a well-prepared and inexpensive range of Sri Lankan and Western breakfasts, rice and curry, plus snacks including lots of sweet and savoury *rottys*.

thought to have imprisoned Sita in the **Rawana Ella Cave**, a few kilometres south of the village. It's a punishing climb up to the cave, including over 600 steps, and sections can be treacherously slippery after rain (there's a very welcome tea shack around two-thirds of the way up). The sweeping views at least partly compensate; bring a torch for the cave.

Ravana also gives his name to the **Rawana Ella Falls**, a little further down the Wellawaya Road some 6km (3.7 miles) south of Ella. The falls are undeniably impressive – a great cataract of water tumbling over a cliff right next to the road – although they're usually busy with passing crowds of tourists, plus plenty of touts trying to flog pieces of pink quartz and the like.

A traditional Sri Lankan lunch

Trains can offer spectacular views

TOUR 7

Dambulla, Sigiriya and Anuradhapura

A two-day excursion into the past, driving from the southernmost point of the Cultural Triangle (Kandy) to the northernmost point (Anuradhapura) with visits to the Dambulla cave temples and the top of Sigiriya en route.

DISTANCE: 250km (155 miles)
TIME: Two days
START: Kandy
END: Dambulla
POINTS TO NOTE: This route connects directly to Polonnaruwa (tour 8) – or if you've seen enough ruins, you could head back south through Kandy and into the hill country (tour 5). For your overnight stay there are plenty of centrally located places in and around Habarana, Dambulla and Sigiriya.

Sri Lanka's so-called Cultural Triangle – the area between Kandy and the great ruined cities of Anuradhapura and Polonnaruwa – served as the birthplace of Sri Lankan civilization and boasts a staggering array of ancient monuments dating back over 2,500 years, including giant stupas, richly decorated cave temples and enormous tanks (man-made reservoirs), capped by the unforgettable sight of the great rock citadel of Sigiriya towering into the sky amidst the arid northern plains.

Dambulla

Depart from **Kandy** (see page 44) and drive north through along the A9 towards **Dambulla**, 72km (45 miles) from Kandy.

Some 3km (2 miles) before Dambulla you'll see the entrance to the **Dambulla Cave Temples** ❶ (charge) on your left. Steps climb up from the ticket office to the temples themselves, passing an enormous gilded Buddha on the way. The temples were created by King Valagambahu, who hid here in the first century BC after Indian invaders had seized Anuradhapura. After regaining Anuradhapura, Valagambahu built the temples to give thanks for the shelter the caves had afforded him. The most impressive of Sri Lanka's many cave temples, the five shrines sit side-by-side beneath a huge rocky overhang, filled with a treasure trove of Buddhist art, including innumerable statues of the Buddha and other deities, plus the finest selection of murals on the island.

If you're already hungry, try the smart modern café at the **Heritage Dambulla**, see ①.

At Dambulla Cave Temples

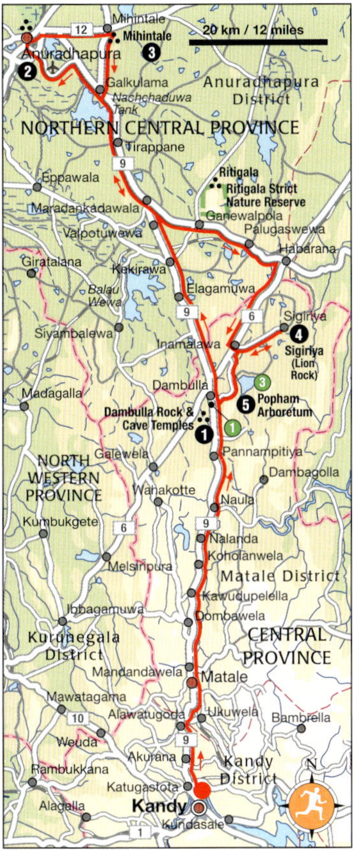

Anuradhapura

It's 86km (53 miles) from here to Anuradhapura along the A9. Sri Lanka's first capital, **Anuradhapura** ❷ was founded by King Pandukhabaya in 380 BC and remained far and away the biggest and most important city in the island's for nearly 1,400 years until the capital moved finally eastwards to Polonnaruwa. Anuradhapura's 113 kings (and four queens) oversaw a great flowering of the arts, producing magnificent palaces, intricate sculptures, ornate pleasure gardens and a sequence of vast stupas built to protect the most sacred relics of Buddhism. Perhaps the most impressive achievement was in irrigation, with reservoirs constructed to preserve the monsoon rains and a complex system of canals and sluices put in place to keep the rice paddies productive.

At the heart of the ancient city, the **Sanctuary at Tissawewa**, see ❷, is a good place to plan an exploration of the ruins over lunch.

Sacred Bo Tree

A good place to start a tour of the ruins is at the **Sri Maha Bodhi** Ⓐ (Sacred Bo Tree; donation). This is the world's oldest historically documented tree, said to be grown from a sapling of the original bo tree in Bodhgaya, India, under which the Buddha himself gained enlightenment. The sapling was brought to Sri Lanka by Sangamitta, the daughter of Emperor Ashoka, in the third century BC, and has flourished ever since, as well as providing the seeds from which almost all the island's other bo trees have been grown. The tree is now encircled by a gold-plated

Buddhist statues at Dambulla

railing amidst a crowd of younger trees, one of its limbs now propped up on gilded supports, while pilgrims feed its roots by pouring pots of water by hand into strategically placed chutes.

On the north side of the bo tree is the **Brazen Palace** Ⓑ (Loha Pasada), which once had a bronze roof, nine floors and is said to have housed a thousand monks, although nothing now survives apart from a dense cluster of some 1,600 stone pillars.

From here it's a short detour west to the **Archeological Museum** Ⓒ, on the shores of the Basawakkulama lake, with numerous fine carvings from the Anuradhapura era displayed in the rooms and garden of a preserved old British bungalow. Exhibits include an interesting model of the Thuparama Vatadage, showing how it would have looked when still in possession of its old wooden roof.

Ruwanweliseya and the Thuparama

Northeast of here rises the huge **Ruwanweliseya** Ⓓ dagoba (stupa), at the heart of the ancient city. Rising over 50m above the surrounding scatter of ruins which formerly comprised the city's great Mahavihara monastery, the dagoba is said to have been built at the behest of the great King Dutugemunu, whose battered limestone statue stands on the terrace alongside. Huge as it looks, the Ruwanweliseya is actually only the third largest of the three great dagobas which rise above the ancient city, although it's also the best preserved and continues to attract numerous local pilgrims as well as foreign tourists.

Continuing north brings you shortly to the **Thuparama** Ⓔ, believed to contain the right collarbone of the Buddha. This is the oldest dagoba on the island, built by King Devanampiyatissa in the third century BC, although its present 'bell' shape is the result of an 1862 reconstruction.

Jetavana Monastery

East of the **Ruwanweliseya** lies the second of ancient Anuradhapura's three great monastic complexes: **the Jetavana.** Centrepiece of the complex is the monumental red-brick **Jetavana dagoba** Ⓕ, Anuradhapura's largest dagoba. Descriptions of this massive edifice tend to attract a string of statistical superlatives: in its original form the dagoba stood 120m high and was at the time of its construction the third-tallest structure in the world, surpassed only by two of the Great Pyramids at Giza in Egypt. It was also the world's biggest stupa and is still the tallest and largest structure made entirely of bricks anywhere on earth, having taken a quarter of a century to build and containing more than ninety million bricks.

The area south of the dagoba is littered with the extensive remains of the **Jetavana monastery**, all carefully excavated and landscaped – most of

An ancient pool in Anuradhapura

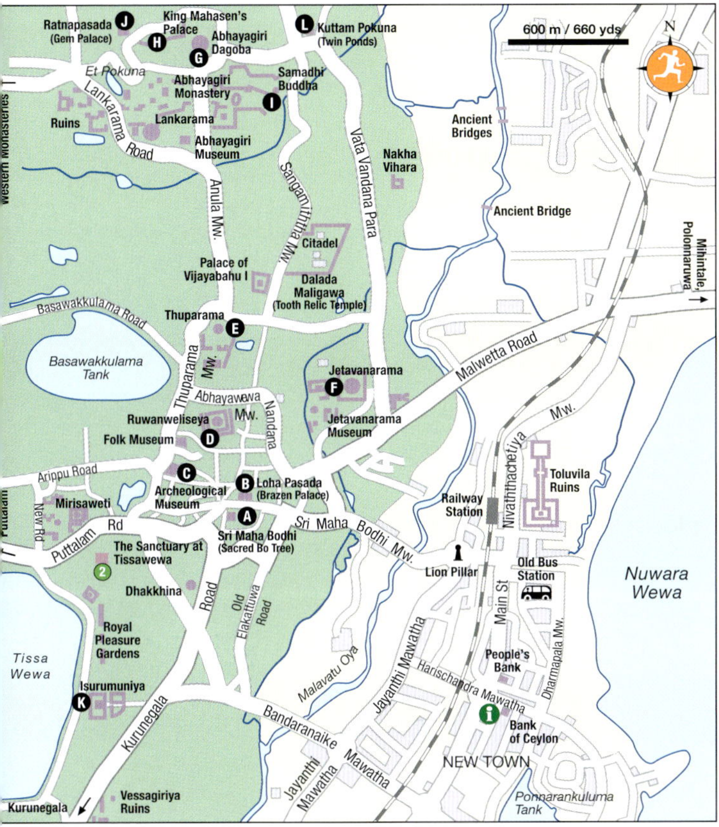

what you see today dates from the ninth and tenth centuries. The monastery would once have housed some three thousand monks and the scale of the remains is impressive, although except in a few places only the bases of the various structures survive. A interesting museum displays some of the precious items recovered from the site, while immediately behind the museum lies a deep and beautifully preserved **bathing pool** and the unusual latticed Buddhist

Elephants guard the Ruwanweliseya

Floral offerings at Anuradhapura

Railing, which formerly enclosed either a bo tree shrine or an image house.

Abhayagiri monastery

North of the Jetavana lies the area of the ancient city known as **the Citadel**. This was formerly the city's royal enclave, home to the king's palace and the temple in which the Tooth Relic was housed – the fragmentary remains of both structures can still be seen.

North of the Citadel lie the remains of the third of Anuradhapura's great monasteries: the **Abhayagiri**. Again the complex is centred on a giant stupa, the **Abhayagiri Dagoba** G, constructed by King Valagambahu (89–77 BC) and standing 74m (243ft) high.

Some of Anuradhapura's most interesting monuments can be found close by. Perhaps the most impressive is the exquisitely preserved **Kuttam Pokuna** H, just east of the dagoba, comprising a pair of linked bathing pools used by the Abhayagiri's monks. Close by, the iconic **Samadhi Buddha** I, is an excellent example of sculpture from the fourth century.

Over on the west side of the dagoba a dense scattering of ruins includes the remains of **King Mahasen's Palace** J, home to one of the finest moonstones in Anuradhapura: a wonderful semicircular doorstep adorned with finely detailed symbolic carvings. Close by, the eighth-century **Ratnapasada** J boasts two of the city's best-preserved guardstones, showing a *naga* (snake) king sitting under a *makara* (dragon) arch, with a flowerpot and lotus stalk – symbols of abundance and prosperity.

Mirisavatiya and Isurumuniya

Assuming you still have time and energy, there's a further interesting cluster of sights in the southwestern area of the ancient city spread along the banks of the **Tissa Wewa Tank**, created by King Devanampiyatissa in the third century BC, and once Anuradhapura's chief source of water.

The most visible landmark here is the **Mirisavatiya dagoba** – very similar to – and only slightly smaller than – the Ruwanwelisaya dagoba. Further west along the lake is the striking **Isurumuniya** K. Here you'll find the famous fourth-century limestone carving of the Isurumuniya lovers: a man and a woman who are said to represent Prince Saliya, son of King Dutugemunu, and a low-caste maiden whom he loved. The woman lifts a warning finger, but the man carries on regardless. Just east of here, the bathing pools of the **Goldfish Park** in the Royal Pleasure Gardens boast cute low-relief carvings of bathing elephants.

Mihintale

Just 10km (6 miles) east of Anuradhapura along the A12 is **Mihintale** 3, revered as the birthplace of Buddhism in Sri Lanka (see box).

A Buddha in the Ruwanweliseya image house

Sigiriya

Leave early the next day and head to the spectacular rock citadel of **Sigiriya** ❹ (Lion Rock; charge), Sri Lanka's single most dramatic and unusual site, with the ruins of one of the city's ancient capitals perched atop a giant red-coloured rock looming over the surrounding plains. The citadel was built on top of the huge rock as an impregnable fortress by King Kassapa (AD 447–95), who had killed his father and feared revenge from his brother.

The foot of the rock is surrounded by ornate gardens of contrasting characters. The well-preserved **Water Gardens** look like a tiny piece of Versailles transported to ancient Sri Lanka, with carefully tended lawns dotted with symmetrically arranged ponds, water channels and diminutive fountains. Beyond lie the wilder **Boulder Gardens**, comprising a small swathe of picturesque forest dotted with huge boulders and quaint rock arches.

Sigiriya frescoes

Past the Boulder Gardens, a steep climb up a brick stairway and spiral staircase leads you to Sigiriya's single most celebrated sight, the so-called **Sigiriya Damsels**. Commissioned by Kassapa in the fifth century, this exquisite mural, perhaps the largest ever attempted, is painted in brilliant colours onto the sheer rock face and features a number of beautiful, bare-chested women, swathed in cloud from the waist down. No one knows whether the damsels were meant to be goddesses, Kassapa's concubines or dancers. Impressive as they are today, it is thought that there were originally some 500 frescoes here, of which only 21 now survive.

Mirror Wall and the summit

Climb past the **Mirror Wall**, a dense spider's web of ancient graffiti left by visitors to the rock over the past 1,500 years, on the way to the **summit**. This involves scrambling through the mouth of a heavily eroded lion and

Mihintale shrines

According to legend, it was at Mihintale – literally Mahinda's Hill – that the Indian missionary Mahinda met and converted King Devanampiyatissa in 247 BC, establishing Buddhism as the island's religion. Mihintale is unforgettable: a sequence of beautiful shrines, stupas and caves strung out across wooded hills and connected by broad flights of frangipani-shaded carved steps, usually clustered with crowds of devout, white-robed pilgrims. Its various shrines are connected by 1,840 steps, all of which must be climbed to reach the summit, where the Ambasthala Dagoba, or Mango Tree Stupa, supposedly marks the place where Mahinda surprised the king as he was hunting.

Murals

Prayer flags

Food and drink

1 Heritage Dambulla
Dambulla;
www.chcresthouses.com; $$$
The smart little modern café at this former rest house provides a convenient pitstop when visiting the cave temples, with above-average light meals plus more substantial Sri Lankan and Continental-style mains.

2 The Sanctuary at Tissawewa
Sacred Precinct, Anuradhapura;
www.tissawewa.com; $$$$
The verandas and dining room of this century-old colonial building retain a sense of rural antiquity. Great for rice and curry, light meals and snacks, although no alcohol is served due to its proximity to the sacred areas.

3 Kanchana Restaurant
Heritance Kandalama Hotel, Dambulla;
www.heritancehotels.com; $$$$
One of several excellent cafés and restaurants at this iconic, Geoffrey Bawa-designed hotel, offering breathtaking views of the surrounding countryside, Sigiriya rock and the Kandalama tank, as well as good food (including lunchtime buffets).

then up a vertiginous metal staircase cut into the rock – not for the faint-hearted, although the view of the water gardens below and surrounding jungle is breathtaking. Amid the foundations and fragmentary remains of the palace is a large tank cut from the solid rock: water was brought to the summit using a typically ingenious hydraulic system driven by windmills.

Popham Arboretum

Drive back to the main A6 highway and head south towards Dambulla for a further 24km (15 miles) to reach a side road east signposted to the Heritance Kandalama Hotel. About 3km (2 miles) along this road is the **Popham Arboretum** 5 (www.nifs.ac.lk/facilities/arboretum; charge), comprising 14 hectares (35 acres) of unspoilt dry tropical forest, criss-crossed by well-maintained walking trails. The arboretum was established in 1963 by British resident Sam Popham as a reaction to the widespread logging of forests. Over sixty years on it has sprouted more than seventy species of precious tropical trees such as ebony, rosewood and satinwood, and attracted plentiful birdlife and other wildlife, making it perfect for a late morning stroll.

The **Café Kanchana**, see 3, at the Heritance Kandalama Hotel is a good spot for a light lunch.

After lunch, return to the A6 to drive northwards back to your hotel to relax by the pool at the end of a fulfilling day out, or turn south for Kandy or Colombo.

Baby elephant on the approach to Sigiriya

TOUR 8
Minneriya and Polonnaruwa

The A6 from Colombo to Trincomalee meets the A11 bound for the east coast at Habarana, making it an ideal starting point for a drive combining the elephant country of Minneriya and the ancient ruins of Polonnaruwa.

DISTANCE: 42km (26 miles)
TIME: A leisurely day
START: Habarana
END: Polonnaruwa
POINTS TO NOTE: It's possible to drive around the ruins at Polonnaruwa but a lot more enjoyable to cycle – bikes can be rented from most local guesthouses and other places around town. After this route, you could spend another night in Habarana, then drive south through Kandy for tours 5 and 6.

From **Habarana ❶**, start early to have the best chance of spotting wildlife in Minneriya and head off along the 43km (27-mile) road from the Habarana junction towards Polonnaruwa. This is one of the loneliest roads in the area and it's not unusual to see wild animals, including deer, monkeys and iguanas, along the way, as well as glimpses of the great artificial lakes (or 'tanks') at Minneriya, Giritale and the ancient capital of Polonnaruwa itself.

Minneriya National Park

Drive northwards to the Habarana Junction to join the A11 to Polonnaruwa and the east coast. At the 32km (20-mile) marker you'll reach the entrance to **Minneriya National Park ❷** (charge), best visited early in the morning or after 3pm to maximise your chances of seeing wildlife. This is one of Sri Lanka's most popular and interesting parks, centred around the large Minneriya Tank and boasting an unusually wide range of habitat types, from grasslands and wetlands to beautiful dry tropical forest.

Elephant gathering

Elephants are the main attraction at Minneriya, which forms part of the elephant corridor that joins up with neighbouring Kaudulla and Wasgomuwa national parks. During the dry season, as rivers and lakes dry up across the surrounding areas and waterholes turn to baked mud, more than 300 elephants converge on the retreating waters of the Minneriya Tank. This massive meeting of elephants – popularly known as 'The

Sunset over Habarana lake

Gathering' (July to October; best during August and September) – is the largest of its kind in Asia, as pachyderms from across the region converge on one of the region's last reliable sources of water, travelling from as far away as Trincomalee to drink, eat, socialise and search for mates.

Polonnaruwa

On the road to Polonnaruwa, look out for unusual yellow road signs warning of land monitors crossing the road – a startling sight as they scuttle away from approaching traffic. Stop for lunch at the rustic **Priyamali Gedara,** see **1**, on the northern fringes of town.

After lunch, continue along the road south. Shortly afterwards the remains of ancient ruins and centuries-old brick walls suddenly come into view on both sides of the road as you approach **Polonnaruwa 3** itself.

Parakrama Samudra

Stretching out along the western side of Polonnaruwa, the **Parakrama Samudra** is a vast reservoir of water created by the legendary Parakramabahu (1153–86), Polonnaruwa's greatest king, who famously proclaimed that not one drop of water should escape into the ocean without it being of some service to man. Even today the ancient reservoir remains a crucial source of water, providing precious irrigation to vast areas of surrounding agricultural land. **EKHO Lake House**, see **2**, is a smart spot for views and refreshments.

Royal Palace

Buy your ticket to the ruins at the excellent **Polonnaruwa Museum A**, well worth visiting before the site itself.

On entering the main archaeological site, you'll immediately see the impressive remains of Parakramabahu's **Royal Palace B** (Vejayanta Pasada). Of the original seven floors, only three remain. A staircase leads nowhere, but its former grandeur can be imagined.

In front of it is the **Council Chamber**. Some fine elephant carvings have been preserved, but even the best craftsmen make mistakes – look for the five-legged

Land monitors roam the road to Polonnaruwa

elephant near one of the entrances.

Nearby are the remains of the **Kumara Pokuna** Ⓒ (Royal Baths), an exquisite stepped bath of cut stone. Underground stone conduits feed it with water from the Parakrama Samudra. Two of the original five crocodile spouts are still intact.

The Quadrangle

Polonnaruwa's densest and most impressive cluster of ruins are concentrated in the spectacular **Quadrangle** Ⓓ, a short walk north of the Royal Palace.

Entering the Quadrangle, your eyes will immediately be drawn to the **Vatadage** Ⓔ on the left, a circular relic house and probably the oldest – and certainly the most beautiful – building in Polonnaruwa. Built by Parakramabahu and subsequently embellished by Nissankamalla, this is one of the most ornately decorated buildings in Sri Lanka, its outer walls carved with friezes. Steps lead up to the central shrine, presided over by four Buddhas, and a central brick dagoba.

Directly opposite the Vatadage is the relatively modest **Hatadage** Ⓕ, once used to house the tooth relic of the Buddha and built according to – unlikely – legend in just sixty (*hata*) hours.

A colourfully painted bus

Minneriya elephants

East-coast season

It's around 85km (53 miles) from Habarana Junction along the A6 to the east-coast harbour city of **Trincomalee** ❹ and the popular nearby beach resorts of Uppuveli and Nilaveli (which offer a great escape between May and October, when the island's west-coast beaches are battered by the monsoon). Trincomalee was the island's main port during the Polonnaruwa era and was subsequently coveted by the Portuguese, Dutch, French and British (not to mention the Japanese, who bombed it in 1942) on account of its splendid harbour, one of the largest deep-water anchorages in the world.

The centrepiece of 'Trinco' (as it's familiarly known) is Fort Frederick, originally built by the Portuguese in 1623, and still boasting its original gateway and a number of well-preserved colonial buildings. This is also where you'll find the revered **Koneswaram Kovil**, the largest of the many Hindu temples dotting the town, perched high above the waves near the top of the dramatic Swami Rock.

On the right of the Hatadage, the unusual **Sathmahal Pasada** Ⓖ ('Seven-Storey Dagoba', although only six remain) has a decidedly Southeast Asian appearance, faintly reminiscent of the Khmer architecture of Cambodia and perhaps showing the influence of architects from Myanmar (Burma), a country with which Parakramabahu established strong links.

Next to the Sathmahal Pasada is the massive 9m (30ft) long **Gal Potha** Ⓗ (Book of Stone), one of the longest and heaviest of its kind in the world. The enormous slab of stone, 1.5m (5ft) wide and over 60cm (2ft) thick, is inscribed with the great achievements of Parakramabahu's successor and nephew, Nissankamalla. An inscription records that the 25-tonne stone was brought from Mihintale, over 100km (60 miles) away, using wooden rollers tugged by elephants.

On the other side of the Hatadage are the fragmentary remains of the **Atadage** Ⓘ, built by King Parakramabahu's predecessor, King Vijayabahu, which also once housed the Buddha's tooth.

The **Thuparama** Ⓙ temple, the only building in the Quadrangle with a roof, contains nine statues of the Buddha. One is broken but others, made of quartz and containing mica, glisten in the light of a candle or torch.

Shiva Devale

Leave the Quadrangle, head north and turn right at the first crossroads towards the **Shiva Devale** Ⓚ, a circular relic house where the *yoni* and *lingam*, symbols of fertility, are worshipped by Hindu women seeking blessings for conception. From here, drive (or cycle) north to the **Rankot Vihara** Ⓛ ('Gold-Pinnacled Stupa'), a colossal

The ancient Vatadage

red-brick dagoba standing 40m (125ft) high with a circumference of 170m (550ft). The remains of the **Alahana Pirivena** (university) and the **Royal Burial Grounds** are located nearby.

Gal Vihara and around

Continue north to reach the well-preserved **Kiri** (Milk) **Vihara** **M**, a dagoba named for the milk-white stucco that once covered the entire dome. Close by, the **Lankatilaka** image house **N** has thick 17m (56ft)-high walls enclosing a headless statue of the standing Buddha.

Across the road is one of the ancient city's undoubted highlights, the **Gal Vihara** **O** (Rock Temple), home to an exquisite quartet of eleventh-century Buddha statues, carved out of solid rock – including a huge reclining Buddha.

Island Garden and the Parakramabahu statue

There's a further cluster of sights around the Polonnaruwa Museum and further south. You don't need a ticket to visit these so you could save them for the following morning to avoid ruins-overload.

Immediately north of the museum, the **Deepa Uyana (Island Garden)** **P** area preserves the remains of Nissankamalla's old royal place.

Drive (or cycle) south along the lakeside Pothgul Mawatha (Bund Road), constructed on top of the lake's embankment. After about 1.5km (1 mile), a small gate on your left opens into a park (daily; free) where you'll find one of Polonnaruwa's most famous relics: a twelfth-century **statue** **Q** of a man holding a scroll, thought to be either King Parakramabahu himself or Agastaya, an Indian religious teacher.

Food and drink

1 Priyamali Gedara
Bendiwewa, 4km north of Polonnaruwa; tel: 071 721 6480; daily; $$
Traditional rice and curry meals, served in the rustic *gedara* (house) of hosts Priya and Mali. The daily lunch spread features as many as twenty seasonally changing curries, cooked over firewood for extra flavour and served with red rice.

2 EKHO Lake House – Polonnaruwa
Polonnaruwa; www.ekhohotels.com/ekholakehouse; $$$$
Beautifully located on the banks of the enormous Parakrama Samudra man-made lake, Polonnaruwa's famous old rest house has now been converted into a smart modern boutique hotel. It remains a good place for lunch or dinner, with a decent selection of well-prepared Sri Lankan and international food – eat either in the spacious dining room or on the outdoor terrace above the water.

Visiting the Gal Vihara rock sculptures

WALK 9
Galle Fort

Step back in time with a morning walk around old Galle, the most perfectly preserved colonial town in Sri Lanka, before heading off for a leisurely afternoon (or longer) on the nearby beach at Unawatuna.

DISTANCE: 3km (2 miles)
TIME: A leisurely day
START: Galle Fort
END: Unawatuna
POINTS TO NOTE: Galle Fort is 116km (72 miles) from Colombo and easily reached by rail or road – the journey from Colombo by road takes little more than an hour if travelling via the modern Southern Expressway motorway compared to around three hours (or more) via the narrow and congested old coast road. From Galle it's a further 5km by road to Unawatuna, and then another 75km (46 miles) to Tangalla (tour 10) or 181km (112 miles) along the south coast to Yala National Park (tour 11)..

One of Asia's most perfectly preserved period pieces, colonial Galle – usually described as 'Galle Fort' to distinguish it from the modern city outside the old town walls – dates back to the period when the island was ruled by the Dutch, who seized Galle from the Portuguese in 1640 and spent the next 156 years fortifying and embellishing the town. Their work remains apparent everywhere, with streets of low-slung colonial villas protected by massive coral bastions, while breaking waves crash gently beyond.

Main Gate

The entire fort area is enclosed within a dramatic ring of impressively solid-looking walls and bastions, first created by the Portuguese and later significantly strengthened by the Dutch during the seventeenth century to withstand enemy cannonballs – while more than three hundred years later they also did a sterling job of keeping the 2004 tsunami at bay.

The principal entrance to the Fort is through the **Main Gate** ❶, overlooking the cricket stadium around 250m/yds from the railway and bus stations. The clock tower looming over the central Moon Bastion was added in 1881.

Church Street

After emerging through the gateway, follow Church Street as it curves east

Galle Fort from above

below the rampart wall. The long, whitewashed building on your right is the **Galle National Museum** ❷ (www.museum.gov.lk; charge), originally part of a complex built by the Dutch in 1684 to house army officers and now home to a few rather lacklustre displays on the history of the city. Immediately past here lies the superb **Amangalla** hotel (see page 95), occupying an imposing three-storey building originally built for the Dutch governor in 1684.

Groote Kerk

On the corner of Middle Street next to Amangalla, the beautiful Dutch **Groote Kerk** ❸ (Great Church; donation) dates from 1755 and is the

A Galle Fort street vendor

Unawatuna

Spread out around a picture-perfect bay, Unawatuna village (5km/3 miles) east along the south coast) is one of Sri Lanka's most popular beachside hangouts. Burgeoning development has significantly eroded the village's former chilled backpacker vibe, although the heart of the village retains an enjoyably homespun and left-field atmosphere by day – with lots of indie cafes, surf shops and craft boutiques – while lively beachfront restaurants and regular beach parties keep things lively most nights. There's also reasonable swimming plus a bit of snorkelling and surfing (although not as good as at nearby Hikkaduwa).

oldest Protestant place of worship in Sri Lanka. The church's detached **belfry**, built in 1701, stands over the road at the corner of Queen's Street.

A little further along Church Street is the squat British-era **All Saints' Church,** topped with a distinctively stumpy steeple which dominates the local skyline. Just beyond this point the stunning **Galle Fort Hotel**, see ①, was created from an old Dutch mansion of 1695, while further Dutch-era colonial villas along the street (and in the side roads off it) have also now been renovated and reopened as smart boutique hotels and upmarket shops – evidence of the tide of gentrification which has swept through Galle over the past two decades, and of the town's sizeable expat European community.

Queen's Street

Retrace your steps for a few yards then turn right down Queen's Street, where the **Queen's House** (opposite the Groote Kerk) belfry boldly displays the date ANNO 1683. Stretching down the street opposite is the sprawling **Great Warehouse**, one of Galle's biggest and most eye-catching colonial buildings, now home to the town's modern but disappointing **Maritime Museum** ❹ (charge).

Built up against the end of the Great Warehouse is the fort's **Old Gate** ❺, which has the novelty of two competing crests: a VOC Dutch crest (dated ANNO MDCLXIX) above the gate on the inside of the fort, and a British coat of arms, added at a later date, on the gate's exterior face.

Walk back through the gate into the fort and skirt round to the eastern corner of Court Square, where the date 1759 etched into a white wall identifies the **Akersloot Bastion** ❻. Rising above its high walls you can catch a glimpse of the top of what's claimed to be the island's first ever breadfruit tree, a species introduced by the Dutch and now found across the island, with its bulbous green fruit proving a popular ingredient in local curries.

South of here, along Hospital Street, the long white building on the

The Maritime Museum

sea-facing side of the street is the old **Dutch Hospital**, now attractively renovated and home to an excellent selection of places to eat and drink.

A block inland, on Leyn Baan Street, is the quirky **Historical Mansion Museum** ❼ (free), comprising several rooms of random bric-a-brac collected by its owner over the past forty-plus years. Local artisans including lace-makers and gem-cutters can also often been seen at work on the premises. The nearby **Royal Dutch Café**, see ②, and **Aqua Forno**, see ③, are both good options if you fancy a drink, snack or ice cream.

The Ramparts

South of here, Leyn Baan Street continues to the seafront ramparts and the 18m (59ft) **lighthouse** ❽ at the Point Utrecht Bastion, built in 1940 to replace the old British lighthouse that burnt down in 1936. Although you can't climb it, you can step up to the top of the rampart wall and walk along the grass embankment – popular with local snake-charmers. On the landside is the white, Baroque-looking **Meeran Jumma Mosque**.

From here, you can walk along the embankment parallel to Rampart Street with the sea on one side and the rooftops of the tiny houses crammed into the fort on the other. Steps lead down from the ramparts to pockets of beach where families splash in the sea and couples snuggle under umbrellas.

Food and drink

① Ropewalk

Galle Fort Hotel, 28 Church Street; www.galleforthotel.com; $$$$

The suave Ropewalk restaurant in the superb Galle Fort Hotel provides a stylish setting for classic Sri Lankan cuisine given a fine-dining makeover, including slow-cooked jackfruit, baked fish in banana leaf and Jaffna spiced prawns.

② Royal Dutch Cafe

72 Leyn Baan Street; $$

A Galle institution, in business since basically forever, this quirkily decorated little café is a great place for a coffee or tea (including the café's signature ginger infusion) plus light snacks including chocolate and coconut sandwiches or more substantial Sri Lankan mains.

③ AQUA Forno

53 Church Street; www.aquafornobakery.com; $$$

Lovely little bakery-cum-café, with a neat little upstairs terrace and a tempting selection of breakfasts, salads, crepes, focaccia and gelato.

After the **Aeolus Bastion**, the ramparts broaden and provide a breezy walk past the **Star Bastion** to the **clock tower** and back to the Main Gate.

Dutch-era architecture

Stopping for a rest

TOUR 10
Tangalla, temples and turtles

Spend a morning or afternoon exploring the countryside around the sleepy beach resort of Tangalla, with glimpses of the area's magnificent coastal scenery and the lush rural hinterlands, with visits to Mulkirigala and Wewurukannala, two of southern Sri Lanka's most interesting shrines, along the way.

DISTANCE: 50km (31 miles)
TIME: Half a day
START/END: Tangalla
POINTS TO NOTE: This enjoyable half-day round-trip combines visits to a contrasting pair of temples, one ancient and the other modern, along with a glimpse of an unusual natural blowhole – and the tour can easily be combined with a rewarding night-time turtle-watch on the beach at Rekawa. The tour can be done either by car or by tuk-tuk – it's a popular excursion and you'll have no problem arranging transport in Tangalla.

Hoo-maniya blowhole

Start in **Tangalla** ❶ and drive west along the coast highway for around 6km. Just beyond Nakulugamuwa, a narrow side road to Kudawela heads off on the left, twisting for 2km to reach the ocean and the unusual **Hoo-maniya blowhole** ❷ (apparently named after the low, booming "Hoo" sound it produces prior to spouting water). The blowhole is formed from a deep, narrow cleft in the cliff which funnels plumes of water up into the air in great jets by some mysterious action of water pressure – it's most impressive during the monsoon (May–September; June is reckoned to be best), when the jets can reach heights of 15m.

From here, continue on through the small town of **Kudawella** to rejoin the main coastal highway, then continue west for another 5km to reach **Dickwella Bay**, with sweeping golden sand. There's an absence of good places to stop for a break past here, so you might want to pop into the pleasant **Dickwella Resort**, see ①, beautifully situated at the western end of the bay.

Wewurukannala Temple

From the Dickwella Resort, head back east around the bay towards Tangalla for just under 1km then turn left, inland, up Beliatta New Road, continuing for 2km to reach the entertainingly kitsch **Wewurukannala Temple** ❸.

Relaxed beachside café

The temple's main claim to fame is its giant Buddha statue (the largest on the island), a 50m concrete colossus constructed in the late 1960s. The Buddha is shown in the seated posture, with his head crowned by a gaudy, polychromatic *siraspata* (the Buddhist equivalent of the halo). Immediately to the rear of the statue is a seven-storey building, which the Enlightened One appears to be using as a kind of backrest. You can walk up the steps inside the building and peer into the Buddha's head.

The temple's main **image house** dates from the late nineteenth century and contains an impressive ensemble of huge Buddhas in various poses. Exit and turn left to reach another image house containing a kind of Buddhist **chamber of horrors** showing the punishments awaiting wrongdoers in the afterlife.

Mulkirigala

Leave the temple and continue north for 10km to the town of Beliatta, then a further 8km to reach the remarkable temple-monastery of **Mulkirigala** ❹ (charge). The site comprises a series of **rock temples** arranged around a dramatic sequence of terraces carved out of the face of a huge rock outcrop which rises sheer and seemingly impregnable for over 200m out of the surrounding palm forests. The temples

Mulkirigala rock temples

Rekawa turtle beach

Some 10km east of Tangalla, the beach at Rekawa is home to one of the most important sea turtle nesting sites in Sri Lanka, visited by five different turtle species which come to lay their eggs in the sand here most nights throughout the year. Local villagers are paid to protect the turtle eggs from poachers, and some locals are trained as tourist guides. Turtle watches are held nightly, run by the Nature Friends of Rekawa (NFR), whose members keep watch up and down the beach for the turtles' arrival. The best time to visit is between April and July, while periods when there's a full or fullish moon are also good throughout the year, both because there are more turtles and also more light by which to see them. The beach is 4km off the coastal highway east of Tangalla, signposted just east of the 203km post. Turtle watches start at around 8pm from the visitor centre (www.turtlewatchrekawa.org; charge).

date back to the third century BC, but were completely restored during the eighteenth century under the patronage of the kings of Kandy.

The terraces

Immediately to the left of the ticket office lies **terrace one**, home to two rock temples and a small dagoba; the unusual structures standing on elephants outside are oil lamps. The second cave here is one of Mulkirigala's best, with vivid Kandyan-style paintings.

Retrace your steps past the ticket office to reach a steep flight of steps leading up to **terrace two** (home to a single rock temple) and then **terrace three**, with four temples ranged side by side, and a small rock pool at the left-hand end.

The third temple along, the **Raja Mahavihara**, is Mulkirigala's finest, with a vestibule paved with old Dutch floor tiles.

Next to the Raja Mahavihara, steps lead up again to **terrace four**, at the very summit of the site. Scramble down the path to the left of the dagoba for a magnificent unobstructed view over a sea of palms towards the hills inland.

From here, continue east for 2km to rejoin the B410 then turn right and drive the final 10km back to Tangalla.

Food and drink

1 Dickwella Bay Resort

Dickwella Bay; www.brownshotels.com/dickwella; $$$

Long-running resort offering privileged views of Dickwella Bay, best enjoyed from the Baywatch Bar, with sweeping coastal panoramas from the top of the resort's beach town. There's also a good, authentic pizzeria plus buffet and a la carte offerings.

A stunning sunset over the coconut palms

TOUR 11
Yala National Park

The jewel in Sri Lanka's wildlife crown, magnificent Yala National Park provides a memorable showcase of the island's fauna, with troupes of elephants, gaping crocodiles and one of the planet's largest leopard populations, offering an unrivalled opportunity to see this most elusive of big cats in the wild.

DISTANCE: 67km (42 miles)
TIME: A full day
START: Hambantota
END: Yala National Park
POINTS TO NOTE: The best way to visit the park is to take an early jeep tour at around 6am to view birdlife, or at around 3pm for elephants. Leopards can sometimes be seen, but sloth bears are elusive. The park is closed most years from 1 September to 16 October, when animals move elsewhere in search of water. This tour follows walk 9 if you take the A2 for 128km (80 miles) east from Galle; alternatively, after tour 6 drive 88km (55 miles) south from Ella on the A23/ A2 to pick it up at Tissamaharama. From Yala, you could continue to the east coast (tour 12).

The most famous of Sri Lanka's 22 national parks, Yala covers a vast swathe of countryside in the southeast of the island beyond Tissamaharama, protecting a diverse range of habitats including scrub jungle, tanks, brackish lagoons and swamps. Much of the park is closed to visitors, but the area which is open has probably the richest and most varied collection of wildlife in the country, and is the best place for viewing the biggest variety of mammals in a single day. Wildlife includes a substantial elephant population, elusive sloth bears, gorgeous bird life and, most famously, a significant leopard population.

Hambantota

Around 50 miles (80 km) east from Galle, the town of **Hambantota** ❶ was the focus for massive development during the tenure of former president and local boy Mahinda Rajapakse, with projects including the construction of a massive Chinese-sponsored port and the island's second international airport (although it sees hardly any flights). Hambantota itself is one of the biggest towns along the south coast, home to Sri Lanka's largest population of Malay

One of Yala's most celebrated residents

Muslims. You'll notice an unusually large number of mosques here.

Hambantota is also known as the island's major centre of salt production, which is collected from the enormous evaporating salt pans that ring the town, and for its curd. Made from buffalo milk, curd is sold from many roadside stalls and makes a delicious treat – look for the strings of clay pots hanging up outside local shops. For refreshment try the **Hambantota Rest House**, see 1.

Tissamarahama

Continuing from Hambantota along the old coastal road, the route passes through a landscape of thorny plants and small shrubs typical of Sri Lanka's dry zone. After 15km (9 miles) the road passes **Bundala National Park**, famed for its aquatic birdlife, although despite its many attractions it is generally overlooked by visitors in favour of nearby Yala. Beyond here, the road gradually turns inland towards **Tissamaharama** 2 (or 'Tissa', as it's usually called), one of the most historic towns in the south. Under the name of Mahagama it formerly served as the capital of southern Sri Lanka during the Anuradhapuran period.

Safari jeeps

If you're overnighting in Tissa, safaris can easily be arranged either through your guesthouse or with any of the freelance jeep drivers who hang out around town – **Ajith Safari Jeep Tours** (www.yalawild.com), based

A green bee-eater

near the clocktower in Deberawewa, is a particularly good option.

There are heaps of places to eat strung out along the main road by Tissa Wewa lake on the northern side of town including the homespun, open-air **Chef Lady** restaurant, which does great seafood, see 2.

Kirinda

To reach Yala National Park, head south towards the coast along the road to Kirinda, 10km (6 miles) distant. At **Kirinda** 3 there's a lovely view of the southern coast from a temple atop a rock. This is the spot where Vihara Mahadevi, the mother of the Sinhalese hero Dutugemunu, is said to have landed after she been cast adrift at sea in a boat as a sacrifice by her father to placate angry gods who had caused the sea to rise, flooding the coast – an ancient legend which perhaps encapsulates memories of an earlier Sri Lankan tsunami.

Signs of human habitation become sparse as the road winds for another 33km (21 miles) along the coast through scrubland, salt pans and swamps. Watch out for peacocks preening themselves, wallowing buffaloes and the grey silhouettes of wild elephants in the distance. Just before the entrance you'll see signs to the increasing number of upmarket hotels now clustered around the park, including the long-running **Jetwing Yala** and **Cinnamon Wild Yala** resorts, see 3, as well as the extraordinary **Wild Coast Tented Lodge**, winner of the prestigious UNESCO Design's Prix Versailles award in 2018.

Kataragama

A 30-minute drive from Tissa, the busy little temple town of **Kataragama** is (along with Adam's Peak and the Temple of the Tooth at Kandy) one of Sri Lanka's three most venerated religious sites, held sacred by Buddhists, Hindus and Muslims alike – even Christians sometimes pop along in search of divine assistance. Assorted shrines dot the town's sylvan Sacred Precinct, the most important dedicated to the god Kataragama, a Buddhist-cum-Hindu deity who is believed to reside here. The whole complex comes to life during the evening *puja* (from around 6.30pm), complete with musicians, dancers and a great clanging of bells, after which the doors of the main Kataragama shrine are thrown open to worshippers. Best of all, visit during the exuberant **Kataragama festival** (held around the Esala *poya* day in July or August), during which pilgrims express their devotion to the god by performing acts including walking across burning coals and piercing their cheeks with skewers – all believing that the god will protect them from pain.

Elephants in the park

Food and drink

① Hambantota Rest House
Hambantota; $$
Engagingly time-warped government rest house with sweeping views of the harbour below and coastal sand dunes beyond. The dining room is a fine old colonial period piece offering a range of reasonably prepared and inexpensive a la carte dishes including fresh fish and the inevitable rice and curry, served in huge portions.

② Chef Lady
Tissamaharama; $$
Homespun outdoor pavilion restaurant serving up a great selection of seafood – either grilled or featuring in assorted curries – alongside a wide selection of other international dishes.

③ Cinnamon Wild Yala
Kirinda, Tissamaharama; www.cinnamonhotels.com/cinnamonwildyala; $$$$
A nice spot for a break before or after a visit to the park – wild elephants and other animals have often been seen wandering through the grounds. Lavish buffet meals are served in the open-sided Tuskers restaurant, or head up to the rooftop Peacock bar for spectacular views over jungle and coast.

Yala National Park

Entering **Yala National Park ④**, you'll pay the usual national park entrance fees, including those for an obligatory tracker assigned by the park to accompany you on your drive. Many trackers are expert wildlife guides and familiar with the best places to spot wildlife (often near waterholes), including herds of deer, buffaloes, crocodiles, sambhurs, monkeys, flying squirrels and birds that migrate from India and as far afield as Europe including painted stork, heron, ibis, green bee-eater, green pigeon and Malabar pied hornbill.

The greatest thrill, however, is the sight of wild elephants and leopards. Large herds of elephants can usually be seen in the park, particularly around waterholes during the dry season. The real highlight of Yala, however, is its remarkable population of leopards, reckoned to be the densest anywhere in the world, with around fifty animals living in the area of the park open to visitors. Sightings of these notoriously difficult-to-spot and largely nocturnal animals are far from guaranteed, but spend a day in the park and you've got a reasonable chance, with animals sometimes seen sat atop the various rock outcrops which dot the park, dangling from the branches of a tree overhead, or sauntering casually down one of the park's dirt tracks.

A herd of deer

TOUR 12
Arugam Bay to Kumana

Drive the stunning coastal road south from Arugam Bay through a beautiful landscape of salty lagoons and dramatic rocky outcrops to the remote religious retreat of Kudimbigala and the revered temple at Okanda, before going in search of leopards and civil war-era hideouts in remote Kumana National Park.

DISTANCE: 86km (54 miles) (not including Kumana National Park)
TIME: One day
START/END: Arugam Bay
POINTS TO NOTE: This one-day tour connects several of the east coast's most memorable destinations and culminates in a trip to the little-known Kumana National Park. You'll need a jeep to explore Kumana. These can be hired at the park entrance, although you might find it cheaper and more convenient to hire one in Arugam Bay for the entire day, especially given that parts of the road to Kumana are unsurfaced and unsuitable for low-clearance cars. Arugam Bay Tours (www.arugambaytours.com) are a reliable option. Finally, there's a complete absence of places to eat along the route. Take some provisions or get your guesthouse or hotel to rustle up a packed lunch or picnic. If travelling with a tour operator, food should also be provided.

South from Arugam Bay

The tour starts in the lively village of **Arugam Bay ❶**, the east coast's most popular beach destination and a long-time favourite with surfers thanks to its world-class waves. Start by heading south down the coastal road, which rolls through rice paddies and scrub jungle as far as the dusty little village of **Panama** (pronounced *Paa*-nah-mah), 12km south of Arugam Bay. This is one of the most beautiful stretches of coastline along the entire east coast, with miles of superb deserted beach and a pair of huge rock outcrops popularly known as **Elephant Rock** and **Crocodile Rock** for their alleged resemblance to these creatures.

The road south of Panama is currently unsurfaced, although the dirt track is kept in reasonable condition. The countryside here is almost completely uninhabited, and very similar in appearance to that of Yala National Park, with extensive lagoons, scrub jungle and huge populations of birds, as well as occasional elephants and crocodiles.

Fishing boats at Arugam Bay

Kudimbigala and Okanda

A further 12km south of Panama, a side road on the right heads inland for 4km to reach the magical forest hermitage of **Kudimbigala** ❷, with hundreds of caves dotted amidst thick jungle enveloping a cluster of dramatically bald rock outcrops. The complex is thought to date back to the reign of Devanapiyatissa, Sri Lanka's first Buddhist ruler, making it the oldest of Sri Lanka's many monastic jungle retreats.

It's possible to walk around the site's main landmarks in just over an hour. From the car park, follow the path ahead of you (keeping the modern rock-top dagoba to your right) into the surrounding woodland, and keep to the track as it squeezes through the trees and between enormous rock outcrops. After about ten minutes you reach the **Sudasharna Cave**, a small white shrine half-covered by an overhanging rock outcrop bearing the faint remains of ancient Brahmi script.

Following the path to the left of the cave leads after another ten minutes up to the **Madhya Mandalaya** ("Plain of Ruins"), with a small dagoba and other monastic remains scattered over a rocky hilltop.

Alternatively, heading right from the cave brings you to the huge **Belumgala**, a towering rock outcrop topped by yet another small dagoba. Rock-cut steps lead to the top, a breathless ten-to-fifteen-minute climb, at the end

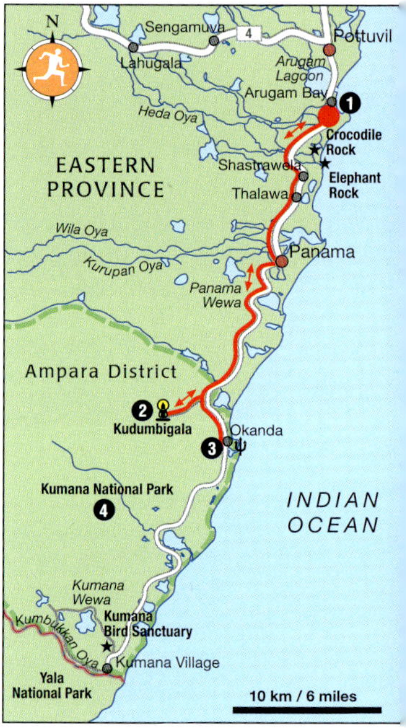

of which you'll be rewarded by one of the finest views anywhere in the east: a vast swathe of jungle dotted with huge rock outcrops running down to the sea, and with scarcely a sign of human habitation in sight.

Okanda

Head back to the main coastal road and continue south for another 2km to reach the village of **Okanda** ❸, home to a major **Hindu temple**, marking the spot where Kataragama (see page

Catching a wave

The Pada Yatra

Every year during May and June, thousands of devout Hindu pilgrims make the gruelling two-month trek, the **Pada Yatra** ("foot pilgrimage") down the length of Sri Lanka's east coast from Jaffna to Kataragama. An extreme exercise in religious dedication, pilgrims leave behind all worldly goods as they make their way slowly south across some of the island's wildest and most remote terrain, stopping to visit 73 sacred sites en route, before finally (god willing) arriving in Kataragama in time for the great Esala festival. Many devotees formerly died every year along the route from assorted privations, disease and animal attacks, and although modern infrastructure and medical facilities have significantly reduced the dangers of the walk, it remains one of Asia's most challenging – and, for those who take part, fulfilling – acts of spiritual devotion.

81)is said to have landed on the island. It's now an important staging point on the overland **Pada Yatra** (see box) pilgrimage to Kataragama.

Kumana National Park

Okanda is also where you'll find the entrance to the little-visited **Kumana National Park** ❹ (formerly Yala East National Park; charge). The park suffered major damage during the civil war years when it served as a Tamil Tiger (LTTE) hideout, but has now been largely rehabilitated and is steadily establishing itself as an offbeat alternative to the adjacent Yala National Park. Kumana sees only a fraction of Yala's visitors, meaning that you'll usually have the place pretty much to yourself.

Kumana Bird Sanctuary

The park's main attraction is the area covered by the former **Kumana Bird Sanctuary**, now incorporated within the park. Comprising the Kumana Wewa tank and surrounding *villus* (seasonal lagoons), this is one of the island's most important breeding and nesting grounds, home to a spectacular array of over 250 bird species and now protected as a wetland area of international significance under the RAMSAR Convention.

Other wildlife includes leopards, some forty elephants, lots of crocodiles and a few extremely reclusive sloth bears. You may also see some of the many cave shelters dotting the area, graffitied with everything from ancient Brahmi inscriptions through to messages left by refugees or LTTE fighters sheltering in the park during the civil war. The park's wartime tribulations can also be seen in the ghostly remains of **Kumana village**, formerly the only settlement inside a Sri Lankan national park until it was evacuated in the 1980s following LTTE attacks.

In the Kumana Bird Sanctuary

DIRECTORY

Our edit of the best hotels and restaurants to suit all tastes and budgets, plus an A–Z of all the essential information you need to know, a quick language guide, and some great book and film recommendations to give you a flavour of Sri Lanka.

Accommodation

Sri Lanka has an excellent range of accommodation in all price brackets, from basic beachside shacks to elegant colonial mansions and sumptuous five-star resorts – indeed staying in one of the country's burgeoning number of luxury hotels and villas can be one of the principal pleasures of a visit to the island, if you can afford it.

Travellers on a budget will spend most of their time in **guesthouses**, usually family-run places either in or attached to the home of the owners. Some of the nicer guesthouses can be real homes from home, with good food and sociable hosts. Rooms at most places of these type of places cost in the region of $12–25.

Hotels come in all shapes, sizes and prices, from functional concrete boxes to luxurious establishments that are virtual tourist attractions in their own right. Some of the finest hotels (particularly in the hill country) are located in old colonial buildings, offering a wonderful taste of the lifestyle and ambience of yesteryear, while the island also boasts a number of stunning modern hotels, including many designed by Sri Lanka's great twentieth-century architect **Geoffrey Bawa**. The coastal areas are also home to innumerable **resort hotels**, the majority of which – with a few honourable exceptions – are fairly bland, populated largely by European package tourists on full-board programmes and offering a diet of very average buffet food and plenty of organised fun.

Sri Lanka also boasts a huge number of luxurious private **villas** (mainly found around the coast) and atmospheric old colonial **bungalows**, many occupying old tea estate bungalows in the hills. All offer stylish and (in the case of tea estate bungalows) often memorably old-fashioned accommodation, although they don't come cheap. There's a great selection online at numerous websites including Boutique Sri Lanka (www.boutiquesrilanka.com), Eden Villas (www.villasinsrilanka.com), Red Dot Tours (www.reddottours.com) and Sri Lanka in Style (www.srilankainstyle.com).

As well as conventional guesthouses and hotels, the island also offers

Price categories

Price for a double room for one night with breakfast:

$$$$ = over $250
$$$ = $150–250
$$ = $50–150
$ = below $50

One of Casa Colombo's luxurious rooms

a vast array of dedicated **wellness retreats** focusing on Ayurveda, yoga or a combination of the two.

The vast majority of places are now bookable online. The biggest selection is on www.booking.com, although many can also be found on rival sites like www.agoda.com and www.bluepillow.com with different (often slightly cheaper) rates. Some more upmarket places only accept online bookings through their own websites, while many others offer a 'best rate' guarantee when booking directly, so compare rates before you commit. You'll also likely pay less when booking directly by phone or email at smaller guesthouses – this is obviously less convenient but saves you money and also ensures that all the money you spend stays in Sri Lanka, where it belongs, rather than being sluiced off into the coffers of a few international online behemoths, who are already rinsing exorbitant charges out of many struggling guesthouse owners.

Colombo

Cinnamon Grand

77 Galle Road, Colombo 3; www.cinnamonhotels.com; $$$

Colombo's grandest hotel, with plenty of five-star glitz and style. In-house facilities include the city's best selection of places to eat and drink, while rooms are attractively furnished, and come with great views over downtown Colombo.

Galle Face Hotel

2 Galle Road, Colombo 3; www.gallefacehotel.com; $$

Famous old colonial landmark in a peerless position on the oceanfront at the southern end of Galle Face Green. Choose between a room in the older Classic Wing or one in the newer and slightly less characterful Regency Wing, all kitted out in neocolonial style and combining modern comforts with traditional decor. There's also a trio of restaurants, a small pool and an attractive spa.

Lake Lodge

20 Alvis Terrace, Colombo 3; www.taruhotels.com; $$

Smooth, modern boutique guesthouse by leading Sri Lankan designer Taru, with stylish rooms in a central but very peaceful location (equally convenient for Kollupitiya, Cinnamon Gardens and Slave Island). The best option in town in this price range.

Paradise Road Tintagel

65 Rosmead Place, Colombo 7; www.paradiseroadhotels.com; $$$$

Luxurious boutique hotel occupying the atmospheric colonial mansion which was formerly the family home of the Bandaranaike family, who have provided Sri Lanka with three prime ministers since Independence. Accommodation is in one of ten gorgeous suites, while facilities include a picture-perfect little infinity pool and a very chi-chi in-house restaurant and bar.

The GEM suite at Jetwing's St Andrew's

Hotel Renuka & Renuka City Hotel

328 Galle Road, Colombo 3; www.renukahotel.com; $$

Smart mid-range hotel in two adjoining buildings (each, confusingly, with a different name), offering modern a/c rooms with satellite TV and minibar – though get a room away from the noisy Galle Road. Facilities include a small rooftop pool, gym, and the good in-house Palmyrah restaurant, known for its excellent Sri Lankan cuisine, including Jaffna-style specialities.

Taj Samudra

25 Galle Face Green, Colombo 3; www.tajhotels.com; $$$$

Set in lush grounds spanning the eastern side of Galle Face Green, this is still one of the nicer places to stay in Colombo (despite being increasingly overshadowed by the new mega-developments springing up alongside). Rooms (some sea-facing) are attractively furnished, if a tad small, while facilities include a health club and pool, plus a good selection of places to eat and drink.

Around Colombo: Mount Lavinia

Mount Lavinia

100 Hotel Road; www.mountlaviniahotel.com; $$$

One of Sri Lanka's most famous old hotels, constructed around the original residence of 19th-century British governor Sir Thomas Maitland. Modern extensions have all but swallowed up the Maitland's former mansion, but the hotel retains enough colonial touches to set it apart from the run-of-the-mill west-coast resorts. Facilities include a superb private beach, Ayurveda centre and decent food either in the main buffet restaurant or the cosier Seafood Cove, offering fresh fish served on the beach.

West Coast: Negombo

Icebear Hotel

103 Lewis Place; www.icebearhotel.com; $$

Sociable and good-value little Swiss-owned guesthouse with ten attractively furnished rooms of various shapes and sizes and plenty of space for idle lounging in the lovely beachfront garden.

Jetwing Ayurveda Pavilions

Ethukala, Negombo; www.jetwinghotels.com; $$$$

Beautifully intimate little boutique Ayurveda hotel, with a range of courses and treatments and an army of therapists on hand to purge your system and balance your *doshas* (although you can also stay here without taking any treatments if you like). Accommodation is in beautiful self-contained bungalows with private garden, each discreetly hidden behind high ochre walls.

Jetwing Beach

Ethulkala, Negombo; www.jetwinghotels.com; $$$$

Jetwing Beach's terrace

Negombo's most alluring address, on its own immaculately manicured stretch of beach at the northern end of the resort area. The superbly designed rooms are elegantly furnished with lots of dark wood and glass-walled bathrooms, and there's also excellent food and a beautiful tree-studded pool.

West Coast: Bentota

Club Villa

138/15 Galle Road; www.clubvillabentota.com; $$$

One of Sri Lanka's most attractive boutique hotels, set in a cluster of gorgeous Geoffrey Bawa-designed colonial-style buildings behind a garden running down to the beach. The place manages to combine style and luxury with a pleasantly informal atmosphere – a perfect place to kill a few days lolling around in the sun and filling up on the hotel's excellent cooking.

Jetwing Saman Villas

Aturuwella; www.jetwinghotels.com; $$$$

Ultra-luxurious boutique hotel superbly situated on the headland dividing Bentota and Induruwa beaches, with wonderful views in both directions and a superb infinity pool built at the edge of the bluff, which seems to hover in mid-air. Rooms come equipped with every conceivable mod con and there's also a fabulous spa.

Shangri Lanka Villa

23 De Alwis Road, Horanduwa; www.shangrilankavilla.com; $$$

Welcoming and intimate guesthouse, run by an Anglo–Sri Lankan couple, with five cheerfully furnished rooms (all a/c; one with a little kitchenette) in an attractive little garden with pool.

Hotel Susantha Garden

Nikethana Road, Pitaramba; $$

Reliable budget option, just behind the railway station and a very short walk from the beach, with pleasant, simple rooms (some with air conditioning) around a shady central courtyard.

Thaala Bentota

Bentota beach; www.brownshotels.com/thaalabentota; $$$$

Formerly the Avani Bentota, this is one of Bentota's nicest – and most expensive – options, in a serene Geoffrey Bawa-designed complex on a pleasantly wide stretch of beach. Facilities include a big pool, smooth spa and very chic rooms boasting wooden floors and huge 40-inch flatscreen TVs.

The Villa Bentota

138/18 Galle Road; www.kkcollection.com/the-villa-bentota; $$$$

Alluring bolthole (formerly known as Paradise Road The Villa), occupying the superb Mohotti Walauwe, a fine old colonial-era mansion which was restyled by Geoffrey Bawa in the 1970s. The whole place is a model of stylish intimacy, with chic but comfortable rooms, a gorgeous pool and lovely gardens running down to the sea.

Sunset dining at Jetwing Beach

West Coast: Ahungalla

Heritance Ahungalla

Ahungalla; www.heritancehotels.com; $$$$

Nestled amid a sea of palm trees, this luxurious Geoffrey-Bawa designed five-star is large but cleverly laid-out to preserve a sense of intimacy, with interlinked buildings backing a huge infinity pool which seems to blend magically with the sea.

West Coast: Hikkaduwa

Asian Jewel

Baddegama Road; www.asianjewelboutiquehotel.com; $$

A real gem of a boutique hotel, set on the shores of panoramic Bird Lake just a few minutes inland from Hikkaduwa. Rooms are decorated in colonial style and set amidst beautiful gardens, and the food is top-notch.

Kandy

The Elephant Stables

46 Nittawela Rd www.elephantstables.com; $$$$

Very stylish boutique hotel, set in a beautifully updated colonial villa with fine views towards the Knuckles Range. There are just six gorgeous and very comfortable colour-coded rooms (plus cottage and luxury tent) in a kind of contemporary country-house style, with vibrant decor, heaps of comfy furniture and a real home-from-home feel. Facilities include an attractive decked pool in the neat garden, a cosy bar and lounge, plus cute little library, with city tours in the hotel's classic cars available on request.

Helga's Folly

32 Frederick E. Silva Mawatha; www.helgasfolly.com; $$$

Marvellously maverick hotel, set in a glorious position high above Kandy. The interior is like a kind of eccentric museum, filled with huge quantities of bric-a-brac ranging from animal heads and colonial photos to Indonesian puppets and huge candles covered in clumps of solidified wax. All rooms are individually decorated with colourful murals. The dispensary bar, cluttered nooks and crannies, laidback service, absence of package tourists, and occasional appearances by Madame Helga herself, are all part of the charm.

The Kandy House

Amunugama Walauwa, Gunnepana; www.thekandyhouse.com; $$$$

One of the island's most magical boutique hotels, occupying a wonderfully atmospheric old traditional manor house tucked away in peaceful countryside a few miles from Kandy. Rooms are beautifully furnished in traditional style, and there's good food and a picture-perfect little infinity swimming pool in the lovely landscaped gardens.

Mcleod Inn

65A Rajapihilla Mw; www.mcleod-inn.kandyhotelsnow.com; $

Get a round in

Kandy's best bargain, perched in a peerless location high above town and with very friendly and super-efficient service from the husband-and-wife owners. The ten a/c rooms are clean, modern and attractively furnished. All come with satellite TV, while two have views to dream of through enormous French windows, as does the dining room. Excellent value.

Queen's Hotel

4 Dalada Veediya, Kandy; www.queenshotel.lk; $$

This venerable hotel is worth staying at for its location, right opposite the Temple of the Tooth, and for its nostalgic value. Rooms are a bit creaky and road noise can be a problem, although rates are excellent value.

The Radh Hotel

30 Colombo St; www.theradh.com; $$$

A welcome addition to Kandy's meagre selection of city-centre hotels, this stylish new place raises the bar significantly, with cool modern rooms and top-notch service. Facilities include a small spa, gym and in-house café, plus the attached Nihonbashi restaurant, serving upmarket Japanese fare.

Hill Country: Nuwara Eliya

Glendower

5 Grand Hotel Road, Nuwara Eliya; www.hotelglendower.com; $$

Small and cosy faux-colonial bungalow hotel in a leafy setting by the golf course. Its nine rooms have polished wooden floors and furniture, and beds with plenty of blankets and quilts. The breakfast room transforms into the King Prawn Chinese restaurant for lunch and dinner, and there's a welcoming pub plus a roaring log fire in the lounge.

The Grand

Grand Hotel Road, Nuwara Eliya; www.tangerinehotels.com; $$$$

This huge old colonial hotel is one of Nuwara Eliya's major landmarks. The imposing exterior and time-warped public areas are a superb reminder of Victorian times, although the rooms themselves are relatively ordinary and expensive compared to the Hill Club and St Andrews.

Heritance Tea Factory

Kandapola, Nuwara Eliya; www.heritancehotels.com; $$$

One of Sri Lanka's most ingenious hotels, occupying a converted tea factory – the exterior has been perfectly preserved but the interior magically transformed into a sleek, modern five-star hotel, combining futuristic architectural lines with lots of old tea-making memorabilia. The amazing setting is another major draw, high up in one of the most spectacular parts of the Nuwara Eliya region and surrounded by miles of tea plantations.

Hill Club

29 Grand Hotel Road, Nuwara Eliya; www.hillclubsrilanka.net; $$$

A room at St Andrew's

Chic decor is a hallmark of Heritance hotels

Set in a 1930s mock-Gothic building close to the town centre, this famous colonial hotel offers a real taste of the Ceylon of yesteryear. The interior is brim-full of nostalgia, with a musty library, casual and residents' bars plus assorted stuffed stags' heads and cracked leather furniture. Accommodation is in neat, slightly chintzy rooms with creaking wood floors.

Jetwing St Andrew's

10 St Andrew's Drive, Nuwara Eliya; www.jetwinghotels.com; $$$$

Nuwara Eliya's smartest hotel, occupying a beautiful colonial country club surrounded by graceful lawns running down to the golf course. The oak-panelled bar and restaurant are pure Edwardian period pieces, while rooms are cosy and comfortable.

Hill Country: Ella

98 Acres

Passara Rd; www.resort98acres.com; $$$$

Gorgeous eco-resort set amid the rolling tea-bushes of the Uva Greenland Estate. Accommodation is in a string of rustic-chic stone-thatched cabanas, perched on the ridge at the top of the estate, with stylish rooms up and down and stunning views of nearby Little Adam's Peak and Ella Rock.

Waterfalls Homestay

Kithalella; www.waterfalls-guesthouse-ella.com; $$

As the name suggests, this place is more like a homestay than a conventional guest house, tucked away just outside Ella village in an idyllic location facing Little Rawana Ella Falls. The atmosphere is very peaceful and intimate, with just three rooms (including one triple/family room), comfortably and colourfully furnished, and communal meals served in the kitchen-cum-dining room or on the lovely terrace outside.

Cultural Triangle: Habarana

Cinnamon Lodge

Dambulla Rd; www.cinnamonhotels.com; $$$$

One of the Cultural Triangle's most appealing places to stay, this stylish five-star hotel occupies an idyllic setting spread out across superb grounds running down to the beautiful Habarana Lake. Accommodation is in spacious, good-looking rooms in a string of attractive two-storey cottages scattered around the grounds, while facilities include a large pool, open-air pavilion restaurant and the Azmaara spa.

Cultural Triangle: Giritale

The Deer Park Hotel

Giritale; www.deerparksrilanka.com; $$$$

Tranquil eco-resort discreetly buried away amidst tropical jungle close to the Minneriya National Park. Accommodation is in stylish individual chalets dotted around beautiful

A four-poster bed at the Fortress

wooded grounds, and there's also a nice pool and Ayurveda centre.

Cultural Triangle: Dambulla

Heritance Kandalama

Kandalama; www.heritancehotels.com; $$$$

One of Sri Lanka's most original hotels, this Bawa-designed establishment offers the ultimate marriage of architecture and nature, clinging to the side of a rocky outcrop and almost completely buried by layers of tropical vegetation. Stunning views of Sigiriya and the Kandalama lake, plush modern rooms, and one of the island's most spectacular swimming pools all add to the allure.

Cultural Triangle: Sigiriya

Back of Beyond Pidurangala – Kurulu Uyana

Pidurangala; www.backofbeyond.lk; $$$

Idyllic eco-retreat set in bird-rich jungle at the base of Pidurangala, a couple of miles from Sigiriya. Accommodation ranges from a trio of colourfully painted little cottages (fan only) through to a pair of impressive two-storey treehouses, open to nature on all sides, while staff rustle up good Sri Lankan food and serve as ad hoc nature guides.

Jetwing Vil Uyana

3.5km east of Inamaluwa Junction; www.jetwinghotels.com; $$$$

The Cultural Triangle's most memorable place to stay – and a remarkable experiment in eco-friendly tourist development. Vil Uyana occupies a large tract of reclaimed agricultural land which has been turned into a mixed habitat comprising sections of marsh, paddy, forest and lake, with expansive wetlands created using traditional Sri Lankan irrigation techniques – a marvellous oasis, wonderfully tranquil and rich in birdlife and other natural attractions. Accommodation is in individual chalets modelled on traditional Sinhalese village architecture but luxuriously appointed inside with all mod cons, while the main building, with restaurant, bar, spa and library, is contemporary Sri Lankan design at its most stunning.

South Coast: Galle

Amangalla

10 Church Street, Fort; www.amanresorts.com; $$$$

Occupying the sensitively restored premises of Galle's famous old New Oriental Hotel, this establishment remains wonderfully faithful to the period character of its colonial predecessor, combining old-world colonial chic with the last word in contemporary luxury – a compelling combination, though at a considerable price.

The Fort Printers

39 Pedlar Street, Galle Fort; www.thefortprinters.com; $$$

Characterful boutique hotel in the very heart of old Galle, occupying

The infinity pool at Heritance Kandlama

Night falls on the Fortress

the barn-like building which formerly housed the town's printing shop. The hotel's five suites are little museum-pieces of Dutch colonial architecture, with creaking wooden floors and high beamed ceilings, the rather austere effect relieved by a generous dash of colourful fabrics and artworks.

Galle Fort Hotel

28 Church Street, Fort; www.galleforthotel.com; $$$

Stunning hotel set in a magnificently converted old Dutch warehouse – like the nearby Amangalla, it manages to combine colonial charm and contemporary luxury, though at a far more affordable price. It also dishes up some of Sri Lanka's best foreign cuisine, with a predominantly Southeast Asian slant – a pleasant change if you have had one too many rice and curries.

Jetwing Lighthouse

Dadella; www.jetwinghotels.com; $$$$

Set on a breezy stretch of seafront a couple of kilometres outside Galle, this Geoffrey Bawa-designed hotel is one of the great Sri Lankan architect's defining creations, with a simple, serene exterior, gorgeously designed rooms and splashes of local colour (such as the remarkable quirky wrought-iron staircase depicting the Portuguese arrival in Sri Lanka). A high-quality choice, with excellent food across its eateries, and heaps of facilities too.

Kahanda Kanda

Angulugaha, Galle; www.kahandakanda.com; $$$$

For a touch of ultimate luxury, the KK offers the feel of staying in a private villa with all the amenities of a five-star hotel. There are just eight suites, all uniquely decorated and located in their own buildings, with stunning views over the surrounding jungle and tea plantations. Relax in the garden, swim in the infinity pool, enjoy a massage or learn how to cook Sri Lankan dishes.

The Sun House

18 Upper Dickson Road, Galle; www.thesunhouse.com; $$$$

This long-established boutique guesthouse is still one of the nicest places to stay in Sri Lanka, set in a beautiful old 19th-century planter's villa on a hill high above Galle, with oodles of period charm and memorable cooking.

South Coast: Koggala

The Fortress

Koggala; www.thefortress.lk; $$$$

One of the south's most luxurious (and expensive) hotels, this striking five-star resort is designed to resemble a supersized version of one of Galle's old colonial-era Dutch villas, magnificently framed between superbly landscaped grounds, a vast infinity pool and the sea. The opulent rooms boast all mod cons, while facilities include a top-notch spa and several excellent restaurants.

Buffet dining at Habarana Village

South Coast: Tangalla

Amanwella

Godellawela Beach; www.amanresorts.com; $$$$

Set on sublime Godellawela Beach (or "Silent Beach", as it's generally known), this utterly captivating if super-expensive resort offers a model of how beach hotels in Sri Lanka should be done, with a stylishly understated, low-impact design which blends magically with the surrounding palm trees and water. The rooms are works of art in themselves, with all mod cons including large plunge pools and superb ocean views through huge French windows, plus a sensational infinity pool overlooking the beach.

Mangrove Beach Cabanas

Hambantota Rd; www.beachcabana.lk; $$

Set on a gorgeous stretch of beach with accommodation in quaint beachside wood-and-thatch cabanas (top marks if you can guess where the bathroom is) and more swanky villas. There's also an attractive restaurant, and night-time turtle watches and free canoes to explore the lagoon are on offer – or take a catamaran trip with a local fisherman.

South Coast: Yala

Cinnamon Wild Yala

2km from the park entrance; www.cinnamonhotels.com; $$$$

Luxurious jungle resort scattered around ten acres of jungle between the sea and lagoon. The huge, beautifully appointed chalets – choose between jungle or beach locations – come with all mod cons and luxe–rustic styling. There's also a vast freeform pool and an elevated observation deck from which to try spotting elephants and other wildlife. Safaris into the national park can be organised here. Beautiful and definitely memorable, but expensive.

East Coast: Trincomalee

Nilaveli Beach Hotel

11th mile post, Nilaveli; www.nilaveli.tangerinehotels.com; $$$

One of the island's longest-running resorts (completely rebuilt after the tsunami) with attractive modern buildings set among idyllic tree-studded gardens running down to the beach, the whole place managing to feel pleasantly intimate despite its size. Rooms are comfortable enough, if rather austerely furnished, and there's also a big L-shaped pool and two restaurants.

East Coast: Arugam Bay

Jetwing Surf

4km north of Arugam Bay, Kottukal Beach Road, Pottuvil; www.jetwinghotels.com; $$$$

Upmarket eco-resort on a quiet and pristine stretch of beach north of Arugam Bay. The twenty semi-circular cabanas are miniature works of art, built using natural grasses, palm leaves, coir and local timbers. All have indoor and outdoor showers, and it's fun to leave the doors open and go to sleep to the sound of the waves.

The Bawa-designed Heritance Kandalama

The Fortress's pool is beautifully positioned

Restaurants

Price categories

Price guide for a two-course meal for one:
$$$$ = over Rs5000
$$$ = Rs3000–5000
$$ = Rs1500–3000
$ = below Rs1500

Colombo

Alhambra

Ramada hotel, 30 Sir Mohamed Macan Markar Mawatha; www.ramadacolombo.com; $$$

Long-running North Indian restaurant (despite the Moorish name), with a range of solidly prepared and reasonably priced standards including Mughlai dishes, biryanis and tandooris, plus plenty of vegetarian options.

Chambers at Park Street Mews

Park Street Mews, Slave Island, www.facebook.com/chamberscolombo; $$$

Chambers brings the flavours of the Middle East right to the middle of Colombo, with a good selection of authentic Arabian fare ranging from Moroccan to Lebanese and including tasty meze, succulent kebabs and sumptuous tajines.

Chutneys

Cinnamon Grand hotel, Galle Road, www.cinnamonhotels.com; $$$

Chic South Indian restaurant with a very original twist, serving up little-known regional dishes and street food from India's four southernmost states – Kerala, Tamil Nadu, Andhra Pradesh and Karnataka. There's a particularly good vegetarian selection, plus meat and seafood mains, all bursting with chilli, tamarind and coconut flavours, served up on traditional metal plates and accompanied by authentically fiery chutneys. Excellent value. Open evenings only.

Gallery Cafe

2 Alfred House Road, off Alfred House Gardens; www.paradiseroad.lk; $$$$

Colombo's smartest café, and definitely one of the places to be seen, with a good range of international cuisine and what are claimed to be the capital's best desserts. Or just come for a drink and the chance to watch Colombo's smart set at play.

Hotel de Pilawoos

417 Galle Rd; www.pilawoos.lk; $

Famous local café dishing up big portions of no-nonsense grub at bargain prices. It's best known for its *kottu rotty* (the cheese version has a dedicated following; best eaten, it's said, after a few beers and washed down with an iced milo) and there are also plenty of burianis and burgers on the extensive menu, plus good fresh juices. Unlicensed.

Egg hoppers and characteristic spices

The Lagoon

Cinnamon Grand, 77 Galle Rd; www.cinnamonhotels.com; $$$$

Colombo's best seafood, served up in a bright glass-sided restaurant permeated with salty marine smells. Choose what you want from the superb display of fish and seafood (including prawns the size of small lobsters), and have it prepared in any one of over 25 different cooking styles, from Sri Lankan and Indian to Chinese, Thai and Continental. There's a lunchtime buffet on Sundays.

Ministry of Crab

Dutch Hospital, Fort; www.ministryofcrab.com; $$$$

Regularly voted one of the top 50 restaurants in Asia over recent years, the *Ministry's* unrepentantly crab-centric menu showcases this famous Sri Lankan crustacean in an array of culinary styles, ranging from the ever-popular chilli crab through to a variety of Asian-influenced styles. Wildly popular, and reservations almost always needed.

Monsoon

50/2 Park Street Mews; www.monsooncolombo.com; $$$

At the heart of the buzzing Park Street Mews drinking and dining enclave, this superb restaurant brings an authentic taste of Southeast Asia to inner-city Colombo, served up in a spacious warehouse-style dining area which wouldn't look out of place in London or New York, and soundtracked by the energetic clatter of wok-wielding chefs in the open kitchen. Food features a wide range of brilliantly authentic dishes from Malaysia, Indonesia, Thailand, Singapore and Vietnam featuring all sorts of regional classics: *nasi lemak*, *pad thai*, *beef rendang* and *pho bo*, to name just a few – all delivered to your table the moment they're ready, adding a dash of street-food spontaneity to proceedings.

Navratna

Taj Samudra hotel, 25 Galle Face Centre Road; www.tajhotels.com; $$$$

Arguably Sri Lanka's best Indian restaurant, specialising in unusual regional specialities from around the subcontinent.

Noodles

Cinnamon Grand, 77 Galle Rd; www.cinnamonhotels.com; $$$

This cool, noodle-centric pan-Asian restaurant ventures into various oriental cuisines, with a particular emphasis on Vietnamese and Japanese dishes, as well as offerings from Thailand, Singapore and China, all beautifully prepared and very reasonably priced

Nuga Gama

Cinnamon Grand, 77 Galle Rd; $$$$

Looking disconcertingly like a real Sri Lankan jungle village in the heart of Colombo, *Nuga Gama's* rustic thatched huts, dotted beneath the branches of an enormous 200-year-old banyan tree, offer an enjoyably offbeat setting for an evening meal in the city. The

A traditional breakfast

Dinner on the terrace

nightly set buffet is also a great place to introduce yourself to island cuisine, with a terrific array of classic local dishes, authentically prepared, laid out in seemingly endless lines of claypot bowls.

Palmyrah Restaurant

Renuka Hotel, 328 Galle Road; www.renukacityhotel.com; $$$

Cosy but unpretentious basement restaurant serving up one of the city's best selections of traditional Sri Lankan cuisine including authentic curries, hoppers, pitta and *kottu rotty*. Also offers a rare chance to sample northern Sri Lankan-style dishes from the city of Jaffna, full of rich, feisty spices.

Tao

Cinnamon Grand Hotel, 77 Galle Rd; www.cinnamonhotels.com; $$$$

Set in the gardens of the Cinnamon Grand, where the trees twinkle with fairy lights after dark, Tao dishes up fine fusion cuisine blending Sri Lankan traditions with Asian and European influences. Mains range from seafood and meat standards to more innovative creations, like the combination plate of red curry chicken, grilled lamb chops and spiced tiger prawns.

Upali's

65 C.W.W. Kannangara Mw; www.upalis.com; $$

One of the best places for Sri Lankan food in Colombo, serving up brilliantly authentic, sensibly priced island cuisine in a simple modern licensed restaurant – and usually rammed with locals as a result. Traditional Sinhalese cooking is the order of the day, with a distinct dash of lively Jaffna flavours (try the signature Jaffna crab curry). Choose from all sorts of dishes including mutton, cashew (*kadju*), jackfruit, fish-head and white potato curries, spicy *rasam* soups, plus hoppers, string hoppers, *pittu* and *kottu rotty*, all served in traditional clay pots.

West Coast: Negombo

Bijou

44 Porutota Rd; $$$

Homely Swiss-managed place offering a tempting menu of excellent Central European dishes such as pepper steak, Wiener schnitzel and fondues (order in advance), plus a range of perfectly prepared seafood.

Serendib

35a Porutota Rd; www.serendibnegombo.com; $$

Large and usually lively restaurant with seating either indoors or in the spacious (if scruffy) garden at the back. The menu features all the usual suspects – rice and curries, devilled dishes, pizza, pasta and a surfeit of seafood – reasonably prepared and served in generous portions.

West Coast: Bentota

Club Villa

138/15 Galle Road; www.clubvillabentota.com; $$$

Even if you're not staying here, it's worth visiting this beautiful little Bawa-designed boutique hotel for a chance

Preparing a prawn roti

to soak up the atmosphere and savour the well-prepared international cuisine in the beautiful garden restaurant.

Golden Grill Restaurant

National Holiday Resort; www.goldengrill.lk; $$

This long-running restaurant looks disconcertingly like a Sri Lankan wedding, complete with dressed chairs, a surfeit of pink napkins and flowers on every table, and a chuntering soundtrack of *baila* (Sri Lankan dance music). Food, fortunately, is better than the decor, with an above-average selection of tourist favourites, including lots of grilled things – fish, prawns, chicken and sizzling steaks – plus Sri Lankan standards and seafood.

Malli's

Taniperuwa Watta, near the Galapata Vihara; www.mallisseafoodrestaurant.com; $$$

Large and unexpectedly upscale restaurant tucked away in a lovely lagoon-side setting near the Galapata Vihara. Seafood takes pride of place, using fresh local catch grilled to perfection, and there are also a few meat and vegetarian options – although not many. Pricey, but a distinct cut above your average Sri Lankan restaurant.

Tuna Tuna

33 Beach Road, by Bentota Railway Station; $$

An unexpected find upstairs amidst a row of shops by the railway station, this smart little restaurant serves up a good selection of seafood and Sri Lankan curries at surprisingly reasonable prices. Grab a window seat – great fun when a train passes by.

West Coast: Hikkaduwa

Aroma

285 Galle Rd, Wewala; $$

Excellent organic Sri Lankan and Indian cuisine (with good veggie and vegan option) including a great rice and curry spread and an unusual selection of traditional ayurvedic Sri Lankan soups. No alcohol.

Asian Jewel

Baddegama Road; www.asianjewelboutiquehotel.com; $$$

Eclectic but excellently prepared range of Western or Asian cuisine, travelling the spectrum from full English breakfasts to Thai chicken curry and Indian specialities, as well as the standard rice and curry – or preorder the house speciality, shepherd's pie. Book in advance.

Spaghetti & Co

644 Galle Road, Thiranagama; tel: 091 227 7042; $$

Soothing Italian-owned garden restaurant serving up great pizza and pasta at very reasonable prices.

East Coast: Arugam Bay

Friends Food Café

Main St; $$

There's a bit of everything at this neat little open-air pavilion restaurant, ranging from hearty breakfasts and burgers

Fish and chips, Sri Lankan-style

through to seafood and rice and curry, all delivered with gusto by the friendly staff.

Pizza Hub

Main St; www.pizzahub.lk; $$

Pizza Hub's thin-crust wood-fired pizzas are amongst the best you'll find outside (or even in) Colombo, made by an Italian-trained local chef and including vegan and gluten-free options.

Cultural Triangle: Around Kandy

Royal Bar & Hotel

44 Raja Vidiya; $$$

Set in what's claimed to be the oldest tavern in Kandy, this gorgeously time-warped venue has bags of olde-world colonial character, sprawling over two floors of an old courtyard building full of period detail and atmosphere. The menu features a short selection of Sri Lankan and international standards – steady rather than spectacular, and at above-average prices, although given the setting you probably won't care. Or just come for a drink!

Sharon Inn

59 Saranankara Rd; $$

The nightly rice and curry buffet (daily at 7pm) at the Sharon Inn guesthouse is one of the best in the island, featuring a fine spread of fifteen or so dishes with the emphasis on unusual local vegetables which you won't have tasted before. Non-guests should reserve in advance on tel: 081 222 2416 by 4pm at the latest.

Vito Pizza

56 Saranakara Rd; www.vitopizza.lk; $$$

The wood-fired pizza at this buzzing rooftop restaurant really is the real deal – perfectly cooked thin-crust offerings served with all the usual Italian toppings you'd expect, plus a few pasta dishes and a limited accompanying selection of beer, wine and cocktails. Generally rammed, so either reserve, arrive early or expect to queue.

Cultural Triangle: Habarana

Magic Food Restaurant

Dambulla Rd; $$

Brilliant little family restaurant serving up top-notch Sri Lankan fare – rice and curry, kotthu and so on – in big portions and at bargain prices. It's also licensed, with cold beers and dangerously more-ish arrack cocktails.

Nuwara Eliya

The Hill Club

29 Grand Hotel Drive; $$$$

The famous dinners here offer a real taste of the colonial life of yesteryear. The food itself is fairly humdrum, but the old-fashioned atmosphere, with dinner served promptly at 8pm by white-gloved waiters in the chintzy dining room, is strangely romantic, if decidedly formal – men are only admitted if clad in the obligatory jacket and tie (available free on loan at the club if you don't have your own).

Themparadu

Upper Lake Rd; $$

A tasty biryani

Bringing a welcome dash of contemporary cool to quiet Nuwara Eliya, this funky little hangout is a great place to eat or just have a drink, dishing up burgers, salads (they say they'll make anything you want), 'boring' fried rice and vegan magic mushroom (we won't spoil the surprise). Also a good place for a drink, with cheap beer and a good drinks selection.

South Coast: Unawatuna

Kingfisher

Devala Road; www.kingfisherunawatuna.com; $$$

Excellent beachfront dining, with candlelit tables on the sands, a chilled vibe and a consistently good menu featuring pasta, wraps, burgers, Thai curries and plenty of seafood. Good bar too.

Thaproban Beach House

Yaddhehimulla Road; www.thambapannileisure.com; $$.

Reliable restaurant with above-average cooking, smooth decor and welcoming service – eat either in the attractive dining room or on the beach. The reasonably priced menu focuses on seafood, with offerings fresh from the day's catch, plus Sri Lankan classics and a few international offerings ranging from pasta to nasi goreng – and the pizzas aren't bad either.

South Coast: Galle

Amangalla

10 Church Street; www.aman.com; $$$$

The gracious old colonial-style dining room at the superb Amangalla hotel is one of the most memorable places to eat in the south. Delicious light meals and soups are rustled up for lunch, while dinner features a mix of top-notch Sri Lankan and international cuisine. Alternatively (and less expensively), come for a superior high tea on the hotel's open veranda.

The Gallean

The Sun House, 18 Upper Dickson Rd, www.thesunhouse.com; $$$$

The restaurant at the beautiful Sun House hotel offers a short but beautifully prepared small-plate selection of pan-Asian dishes ranging from Filippino-style barramundi to Korean fried tofu, plus a great drinks list and sumptuous Sri Lankan and western breakfasts.

Indian Hut

54 Rampart St; $

Inexpensive, enjoyably no-frills Indian café occupying a breezy upstairs terrace overlooking the ramparts and sea. Food features a decent range of Indian, Pakistani and Chinese dishes including tandoori kebabs and breads in the evenings from 6pm. Unlicensed.

Wijaya Beach Restaurant

Thalpe; www.wijayabeach.com; $$$

Always lively with local expats, this smooth beachfront restaurant-bar is usually packed out from lunchtime onwards. Food includes a creative range of daily specials, excellent desserts and the south coast's best wood-fired pizza, as well as a good wine and cocktail list.

A fine rice and curry spread

Fresh chillis for heat

Essentials

Accessible travel

Awareness of the needs of people with disabilities remains extremely low in Sri Lanka, and there's virtually no provision for travellers with mobility issues. Few hotels, restaurants or tourist sites are wheelchair-accessible, although there are plenty of one-storey guesthouses that might be usable – though more by accident than design. Public transport is enough of a challenge for able-bodied passengers, and completely useless for wheelchair users, so you'll need your own vehicle and a driver who is sympathetic to your needs – and even then the lack of specially adapted vehicles can make getting in and out difficult. Pavements – where they exist – are generally uneven, full of potholes and protected by high kerbs, while the anarchic traffic presents obvious dangers to those with only limited mobility.

Admission charges

Entry fees to state-run attractions, including national parks and ancient monuments, are relatively expensive compared to other costs in Sri Lanka. Entrance fees to the main sites in the Cultural Triangle are particularly pricey – $30 at Sigiriya, for example, and $25 at Polonnaruwa and Anuradhapura – while national parks generally work out even more expensive once you've factored in the various admission charges, plus the cost of hiring the obligatory jeep and park tracker. Exact costs vary, but visiting Yala (for example) as a couple costs around $40 per person, plus the cost of the jeep. There is no charge at most temples apart from a few of the more famous and touristed places – most notably Kandy's Temple of the Tooth and the Dambulla Cave Temples.

Age restrictions

To qualify for reduced entry charges, children need to be under 12. To drive you must be over 18; to drink, at least 18.

Budgeting

It's still possible to find double rooms in simple family guesthouses for as little as $10 a night, and to get a meal in a cheap or local tourist café for under $5. Realistically, however, you'll be looking at a minimum of around $40–50 per day per person in order to guarantee comfortable lodgings and decent food (and drink), while the sky's the limit if you wish to sample the island's more luxurious hotels and hire your own transport.

Carbon offsetting

Air travel produces a huge amount of carbon dioxide and is a significant

Buddha at the Seema Malaka, Colombo

contributor to global warming. If you would like to offset the damage caused to the environment by your flight, a number of organisations do this, using online 'carbon calculators', which tell you how much you need to donate. In the UK travellers can visit www.climatecare.org or www.carbonneutral.com; in the US log on to www.climatefriendly.com.

Children

Sri Lankans adore children and make a great deal of fuss over them. Baby food and nappies are available in major supermarkets but are relatively expensive in Sri Lankan terms.

Clothing

Cottons and light natural fabrics such as linen are ideal in the lowland heat. Skimpy skirts and brief shorts are not considered respectable (except in tourist hotels and adjacent beach areas), and will attract stares and (for women) potentially a certain amount of hassle. For women, loose cotton skirts or trousers and tops, and a long dress or skirt and long-sleeved blouse for visiting temples are ideal. Men will feel comfortable in cotton trousers or shorts and a T-shirt. For climate details, see page 12.

Crime and safety

The political situation in Sri Lanka remains potentially volatile in the aftermath of the economic crisis and ongoing communal tensions, and it's always worth checking the current situation before travelling. An underlying threat from terrorism remains (as proved by the tragic 2019 Easter Bombings), while security forces maintain a visible presence, particularly in the north and in militarily or politically sensitive parts of Colombo.

These threats apart, Sri Lanka is generally a reassuringly safe country – although women travelling without a male companion may suffer harassment. Levels of petty crime are far lower than in many other Asian countries, and violent attacks against tourists are relatively infrequent. Nevertheless, it pays to exercise caution and obey common-sense rules. Never flash valuables or leave them lying around; do not let your credit card out of your sight when making payments; avoid dark and deserted beaches at night; and do not accept lifts from strangers.

The most obvious safety hazard in Sri Lanka is traffic: the island has an abysmal record of road-related accidents and you should always stay alert when there's traffic around – vehicles often behave in unexpected and potentially dangerous ways. If you're cycling, take extra care.

Swimming is another potential hazard. Dozens of locals and the occasional tourist are drowned every year. If swimming off an unfrequented

Sri Lankan flag

beach, always check local advice and make sure someone knows you're in the water. And never swim under the influence of alcohol.

Drugs are a problem in some coastal areas. Do not get tangled up in buying/selling/using them or get involved with those who do: it is illegal and dangerous.

The following websites publish up-to-date travel advisories: www.gov.uk/foreign-travel-advice, www.travel.state.gov, and www.smartraveller.gov.au.

Customs

If you are bringing in over US$15,000 in cash or traveller's cheques, or valuable gems and jewellery, this should be declared at customs on arrival to avoid problems when leaving. Duty-free allowances when entering Sri Lanka allow you to bring 1.5 litres of spirits, two bottles of wine, and perfume in a quantity for personal use. Note that you are not allowed to bring duty-free cigarettes into the country. Drugs are illegal, and possession could carry the death penalty.

On departure

Customs officers may check your luggage for items being taken out of the country without a permit. The export of 'antiques' (defined as anything over fifty years old) is prohibited without a special licence, as is the export of native fauna and flora.

Technically you're not allowed to export more than Rs.250 in Sri Lankan currency. If you want to convert rupees back into foreign currency, you'll need to produce the forex transaction receipts showing where you originally changed your money.

Electricity

Round three-pin **sockets** are the norm, although a lot of more upmarket hotels have UK-style square three-pin sockets, while combination sockets accepting both round- and square-pin plugs are increasing common. Adaptors for UK-style plugs are cheap and widely available; for any other type of plug it's a good idea to bring your own. Power cuts, once frequent, are now uncommon, while a lot of places have their own generators.

Embassies and high commissions

Australia and New Zealand 21 Gregory's Road, Colombo 7; http://srilanka.embassy.gov.au
Canada 33A 5th Lane, Colombo 3; http://canadainternational.gc.ca/sri_lanka
UK; 389 Bauddhaloka Mawatha, Colombo 7; http://gov.uk/world/sri-lanka
USA 210 Galle Road, Colombo 3; http://lk.usembassy.gov

Emergencies

Fire and Ambulance: 110

A cow investigates some curd

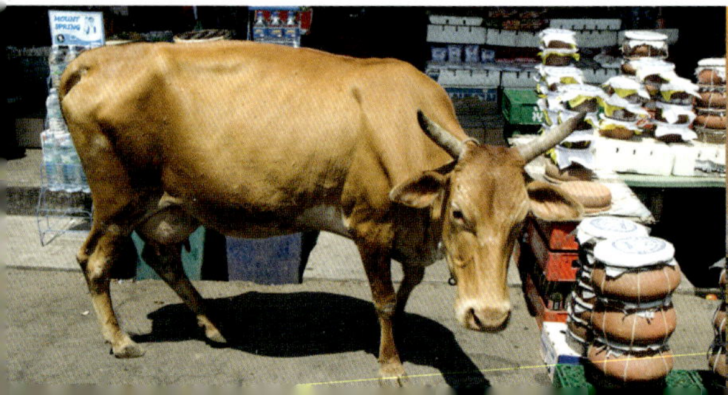

Police: 119 (in Colombo), 118 (elsewhere on the island)

Etiquette

Few Sri Lankans use cutlery, most picking up food with their hands, although visitors may feel more comfortable using a spoon and fork. Food should be handled with the right hand only, as the left is considered unclean. When handing objects to another person, either the right hand or both hands should be used.

Away from the beach, wearing torn T-shirts, skimpy skirts, transparent clothing or displaying bare shoulders is considered highly improper, especially in temples, religious sites or in the presence of monks. When entering holy areas, it is customary to remove your shoes and walk barefoot within the designated area. (This also applies to people's homes.) Women should wear long skirts or loose trousers and a modest blouse, or a loose cotton dress. Men should wear long trousers. Even ancient ruined temples in archaeological sites are still considered sacred, and should be treated as such.

Public displays of physical affection should be avoided.

When invited to a home, it is customary to bring fruit, tea or biscuits or some other small gift. Small presents from one's home country are very much appreciated.

Courtesy is an inherent part of Sri Lankan culture, and one which you should reciprocate. The loss of temper and raising of voices will cause offence, and is very unlikely to further your cause, whatever it is. Many Sri Lankans habitually ask personal questions of all foreigners they meet: you will regularly be asked your country of origin, possibly followed by your age, marital status and number of children. Although such questioning by strangers might be considered intrusive in Western societies, in Sri Lanka these are ordinary questions and simply reflect the emphasis locals place on family life. You may also find yourself being stared at every now and then – not something that's considered rude in the same way as it is in the West.

Waggling the head from side to side is not a negative gesture but a slightly ambiguous gesture meaning either yes, or at least that the matter is being considered.

Green issues

Sri Lanka is one of the world's most biodiverse islands, and **eco-tourism** is beginning to play an increasingly major role in the island's tourism industry. The island has some splendid eco-lodges and eco-oriented hotels; far away the biggest and best eco-tourism tour operator is Jetwing Eco Holidays (www.jetwingeco.com).

Birdwatching is well established, and even if you've never previously looked at a feathered creature in your life, the island's outstanding

Stilt fishermen

Mural in Anuradhapura

range of colourful birdlife can prove surprisingly fascinating. A number of companies run specialist tours, while bird-spotting usually forms a significant part of trips to the island's national parks – although you'll see unusual birds pretty much everywhere you go, even in the middle of Colombo.

Elephants can be seen in virtually every national park in the country as well as at the Pinnewala Elephant Orphanage, the nearby Millennium Elephant Foundation and Elephant Freedom Project, and at the Elephant Transit Home attached to Uda Walawe National Park. For leopards, the place to head for is Yala National Park (with Wilpattu another possibility), while whale-watching trips start from Mirissa, just down the coast, and from Uppuveli on the east coast. There's also superb dolphin-watching at Kalpitiya (plus the chance of seeing more whales). Sri Lanka is also an important nesting site for **sea turtles**; turtle watches are run nightly at the villages of Kosgoda and Rekawa.

Health

Inoculations

No proof of immunisations is required when entering Sri Lanka unless you recently have passed through a country deemed to be at risk of yellow fever transmission. It is, however, advisable to ensure your immunisation for tetanus is up to date. You may also consider getting inoculated for hepatitis A and B, while some travellers also get jabs for rabies and Japanese encephalitis. Always take professional medical advice before departure. Note that all restrictions relating to **Covid-19** had been lifted at the time of writing, and no proof of vaccination is currently required.

Malaria has now been officially eradicated from Sri Lanka, but the risk of contracting the mosquito-borne dengue fever remains very real, especially during the monsoon along the west coast, and particularly in Colombo. There's no vaccine for dengue fever, so it's important to avoid getting bitten.

Healthcare and insurance

The Sri Lankan health service does not provide free treatment for visitors, so having your own medical insurance is vital.

Hospitals

Private doctors and good private hospitals are to be found in Colombo and tourist areas. The medical care at Colombo's private hospitals, centred around Nugegoda, is excellent and inexpensive. These include the **Apollo** (www.apollohospitals.lk); the **Nawaloka** (www.nawaloka.com); and **Kings Hospital** (www.kingshospital.lk). Other reputable

National Day festivities in Negombo

hospitals include the **Ruhunu** Hospital (www.ruhunuhospital.lk) in Galle and the Asiri Hospital (www.asirihealth.com) in Kandy.

Pharmacies

Every town has several pharmacies and most Western medicines are available, alongside many Indian substitutes. The Colombo branch of the state-run Osu Sala Pharmacy (255 Dharmapala Mawatha, Colombo 7; tel: 011-269 4716) is open 24 hours.

Hours and holidays

Hours

Government offices, including post offices, and businesses observe a five-day working week, opening Monday to Friday from around 8.30 or 9.30am and closing around 4.30 or 5.30pm. Banks open Monday to Friday from 8 or 9am until 1 or 3pm; some branches also open on Saturday mornings. All shops and banks close on public holidays. Most branches of Keells and Cargills supermarkets are open 8am–8pm every day (some stay open until 10pm). In small towns, the shopping hours depend on the shop owner; many open late and on Sunday.

Public holidays

Most public and *Poya* (full moon) holidays follow the lunar calendar, with exact dates changing annually. There are three public holidays with fixed dates: Independence Day (4 February); Labour Day (1 May); and Christmas Day (25 December).

The Muslim holidays of Id-Ul-Fitr (Ramadan Festival Day), Id-Ul-Allah (Haj Festival Day) and Milad-Un-Nabi (Holy Prophet's Birthday) are also national holidays celebrated on different days each year, according to the cycles of the Muslim calendar.

Other holidays usually occur in the following months:

January: Tamil Thai Pongal, Duruthu Poya
February: Navan Poya
March: Mahasivarathri, Medin Poya
March/April: Good Friday
April: Sinhalese/Tamil New Year (2 days), Bak Poya
May: Vesak Poya (2 days)
June: Poson Poya
July: Esala Poya
August: Nikini Poya
September: Binara Poya
October: Vap Poya
October/November: Deepavali
November: Il Poya
December: Unduvap Poya

Language

The main language is Sinhala, spoken by around 75 percent of the population. Tamil is the first language of around 25 percent (including many Muslims). English serves as the language of business and tourism

Sri Lankan banknotes

and is spoken well by around 20 percent of the population, while many more can communicate adequately. Sinhala-speakers generally respond to foreigners' attempts to speak their language with incomprehension and prefer to practise their English instead. See page 116 for some helpful phrases in Sinhala and Tamil.

LGBTQ+ travellers

Homosexuality is illegal in Sri Lanka, so discretion is advised.

Media

Newspapers

Sri Lanka has three daily English newspapers and two Sunday newspapers with island-wide circulation; these are mainly available from stalls and pavement sellers. The *Daily News* (www.dailynews.lk) and the *Sunday Observer* (www.sundayobserver.lk) are state-controlled and thus serve as mouthpieces for the government. Independent newspapers include *The Island* and *Sunday Island* (www.island.lk), and the *Daily Mirror* (www.dailymirror.lk) and its sister publication the *Sunday Times* (www.sundaytimes.lk).

Radio

There are several English-language radio stations churning out mainstream pop music and cheesy chat. The best is TNL Rocks (99.2 FM); others worth a listen are Yes FM (100.8 FM; www.yesfmonline.com) and Sun FM (98.7 FM; www.sunfm.lk).

Television

Sri Lankan television is unlikely to take up much of your time; both state and private channels broadcast mainly in Sinhala or Tamil, and what little English-language programming there is tends to be fairly dire. Satellite television is available island-wide with international news channels.

Money

Currency

The national currency is the Sri Lankan rupee. Coins come in denominations of one, two, five and 10 rupees, and notes in denominations of 20, 50, 100, 500, 1,000, 2,000 and 5,000 rupees.

Credit cards

Most mid- and upper-range hotels, restaurants and shops accept credit cards. Visa and MasterCard are widely accepted; American Express and Diners Club less so. Be careful of credit card copying and don't allow your card out of your sight.

ATMs

All major towns across the island have at least a couple of ATMs that accept foreign Visa and/or MasterCard.

Policeman

Tipping

Most hotels and restaurants add a 10 percent service charge to the bill, but you may wish to leave a tip if a service charge isn't included – and indeed even if it is, since there's no guarantee the additional service charge will find its way to the person who actually served you. Chauffeurs and guides will also expect to be tipped somewhere in the region of US$5–10 per day, depending on their skills and helpfulness. Guides who show you around temples will expect a small tip, but don't give money directly to monks (who aren't meant to handle cash); place it in a donation box instead.

Police

Sri Lankan police are generally friendly with foreigners, but if you have a problem or need to report a crime, it is best to take a Sinhala-speaking local with you. There are tourist police offices in a few towns, but these aren't generally much better than ordinary police. If you have anything stolen and want to make an insurance claim, you will need a police report.

Post

When sending airmail letters or cards with stamps, make sure that they are franked in front of you at the post office counter. International courier services include the following:

DHL 307 Galle Road, Colombo 3, tel: 074 049 9897
FedEx 340 Galle Road, Colombo 3, tel: 011 438 4792

Religion

There are four major religions in Sri Lanka: Buddhism (practised by roughly 70 percent of the population), Hinduism (12.5 percent), Christianity (7.5 percent) and Islam (10 percent). Almost all Sinhalese are Buddhist (there are also a small number of Christian Sinhalese). The majority of Tamils are Hindu, though there are also significant numbers of Tamil Christians.

Smoking

You can generally smoke when dining out of doors, on a hotel's open-air terrace or in a restaurant's garden, as well as in pubs, bars and casinos.

Telephones

There are several mobile-phone service providers including Dialog (www.dialog.lk), Mobitel (www.mobitel.lk), Airtel (www.airtel.lk) and Hutch (www.hutch.lk); Dialog has significantly better coverage island-wide than any other network; Hutch is said to be the worst. You can get a mobile signal pretty much everywhere on the island apart from a few remote rural locations. Cheap local prepaid sim cards can be bought

Pettah temple

Post your letters here

on arrival at the airport and at phone shops around the country. The international dialling code to contact a number in Sri Lanka is 00 94.

Time Zone

Sri Lanka is 5.5 hours ahead of Coordinated Universal Time UTC (Greenwich Mean Time; GMT), so 5.5 hours ahead of GMT in winter, and 4.5 hours in summer. Sri Lanka is 4.5 hours behind Australia in winter and 5.5 hours in summer; or 10.5 hours ahead of New York in winter, and 9.5 in summer.

Toilets

Public toilets are virtually non-existent: in an emergency, head for the nearest hotel or decent restaurant. You might also want to carry some toilet paper in case none is available.

Transport

Airports – arrival and departure

Sri Lankan Airlines (airline code UL – or 'usually late' as the local joke goes) operates daily non-stop flights between Colombo and London Heathrow. Emirates (www.emirates.com), Qatar Airways (www.qatarairways.com), Etihad (www.etihadairways.com) and Oman Air (www.omanair.com) all offer one-stop flights from Heathrow via their home cities in the Gulf, and are generally much more comfortable than Sri Lankan flights. Travelling **from Ireland**, you can either make your way to Heathrow and pick up an onward connection there, or fly from Dublin via one of the three Gulf cities that have direct connections with Colombo, currently Dubai (Emirates), Abu Dhabi (Etihad) and Doha (Qatar Airways).

The flight from North America to Sri Lanka takes around twenty hours minimum, necessitating at least one change of plane. There are numerous one-stop routes via the Gulf from east coast cities including New York, Boston, Washington and Toronto with Emirates, Etihad and Qatar, as well as other major US hubs including Chicago, Atlanta, Dallas, Orlando and Miami. Travelling **from the west coast**, the most direct routes go via east or southeast Asia, stopping in Hong Kong, Kuala Lumpur, Singapore, Bangkok, Shanghai or Guangzhou, all of which have nonstop connections on to Colombo.

Colombo International Airport is bright and usually functions smoothly; there are duty-free shops for arriving passengers after immigration. After emerging from customs there is a lobby with banks (including ATMs), hotel and taxi counters. You can book a taxi to Colombo there for about US $20. Alternatively, catch a tuk-tuk to nearby Averiwatte bus station, from where onward buses run to Colombo, Kandy and Negombo,

Truck bearing a heavy load

although it's a slow and crowded experience, and not great if you've just stepped off a long-haul flight.

Public transport

Bus. Buses reach pretty much every town or village of any significance anywhere on the island, though services are often slow, crowded and uncomfortable. Government buses (usually painted red or orange) are incredibly cheap but stop absolutely everywhere and usually get horribly packed – best avoided except for very short journeys. Private buses come in various standards and sizes – from big old rust buckets which are similar in speed, cost and comfort to government buses, ranging up through 'semi-express' and 'express' services, which tend to make fewer stops and thus reach destinations a bit faster. The fastest vehicles, called 'inter-city expresses', usually have air-conditioning, tinted windows and padded seats. These make only limited stops and don't accept standing passengers (at least in theory) and go pretty fast, sometimes recklessly so.

Train. Sri Lanka's antiquated railway system offers a charming – if slow – way of getting around the island, especially on the scenic hill-country line. Fares are low, though carriages can often get ridiculously overcrowded, and delays are the norm rather than the exception. There are three main lines starting from Colombo: the Coast Line runs north to Negombo and Puttalam and south to Galle and Matara; the Main Line goes east, via Kandy, to Nanu Oya and Badulla; and the Northern Line goes via Anuradhapura to Vavuniya. A side branch of the Northern Line goes to Trincomalee, while another goes to Polonnaruwa and Batticaloa. For timetables visit www.railway.gov.lk. Tickets for reserved seating on major routes often sell out weeks in advance so it's best to book these online before arrival. There are a number of websites currently available although the situation is evolving rapidly. Check the excellent www.seat61.com for latest information on the various booking sites currently available and how they work.

Tuk-tuks and taxis

Tuk-tuks Motorised rickshaws (also known as tuk-tuks, trishaws, three-wheelers or just 'taxis') can be found everywhere in Sri Lanka and offer the most convenient way of making short journeys. They can also sometimes be useful for longer journeys in places which lack public transport. These noisy little vehicles can travel at surprising speed through busy traffic, and offer a fun – if sometimes slightly nerve-wracking – way of getting around. Rickshaws aren't metered and you'll need to agree the fare before setting off, and be prepared to bargain. Rickshaw drivers vary enormously by how much they'll try to overcharge

Rail is a charming way to explore Sri Lanka

you: many are fairly honest, though a few are complete rogues. You'll usually pay a bit more in big cities like Colombo and Kandy, and less in more rural areas; the more touristy the area you're in, the more you're likely to need to barter to get a reasonable fare. It's also a good idea to have the correct change for your journey, since rickshaw drivers often claim not to have any change, in the hope that you'll let them keep the difference.
Taxis. There are plenty of taxis in Colombo – often only slightly more expensive than a tuk-tuk, and a lot more comfortable. The cheapest option is to book via the PickMe or Uber apps. There are also numerous radio-cab services – the reliable Kangaroo Cabs (tel: 011 2 588 588, www.2588588.com) is the biggest and best. Taxis can also be hired for longer intercity journeys – try Uber for the cheapest rates.

Driving

Sri Lanka's anarchic traffic and idiosyncratic road rules make driving a challenge for foreigners. If you don't absolutely have to drive, the best option is to hire a car with a driver – which is often no more expensive than hiring a self-drive car. If you're determined to drive, you'll need an international driving licence, plus an additional permit (around US $22, issued on the spot) from the Automobile Association of Ceylon (tel: 011 755 5557), 3rd floor, 40 Sir Macan Markar Mawatha, just off Galle Face Green in Colombo. Reliable **car hire companies** include Malkey (www.malkey.lk) and Casons Rent-A-Car (www.casons.lk), both of which have a good range of cars at competitive rates, with or without a driver.

If you're planning to tour the island by car it's best to book a tour ahead of arrival with a reputable tour agency. The best established local operator is **Jetwing Travels** (www.jetwingtravels.com), while Sri Lanka specialists **Red Dot Tours** (www.reddottours.com) are another good option. Recommended cheaper alternatives include **Sri Lanka Driver Tours** (www.srilankadrivertours.com) and **Destination Sri Lanka** (www.dsltours.com).

Visas and passports

Nationals from all countries apart from the Maldives and Singapore now require a visa, or 'ETA' (Electronic Travel Authorization) to visit Sri Lanka. These can either be obtained online before you arrive at www.eta.gov.lk or on arrival at the airport. The fee for a tourist visa is currently $50 if bought in advance online, or $60 if bought on arrival. The visa is valid for thirty days and for two entries. Passports must be valid for six months after arrival.

In Sri Lanka, the thirty-day tourist visa can be **extended** to six

Negombo fishing vessels at sea

months online at www.eta.gov.lk. Alternatively, it can be extended three times up to a maximum of 270 days (sixty days on first extension, ninety days on second and third) by visiting the Immigration Service Centre (Mon–Fri 8.30am–1.30pm; tel: 1962, www.immigration.gov.lk) at the Department of Immigration, Sri Subhithipura Road, Battaramula, Colombo. You can extend your visa as soon as you get to Sri Lanka; the thirty days included in your original visa is included in the initial ninety-day extension, giving you 120 days. You'll need to bring one passport photo. Conditions for extensions are an onward ticket and proof of sufficient funds, although a credit card will probably suffice. Fees are around $55 per extension. Expect the whole procedure to take an hour or two.

Websites

As well as the useful websites listed elsewhere in this book, the following may also be of interest:

www.srilanka.travel – Official website of the Sri Lanka Tourism Promotion Bureau.

www.withanage.tripod.com – Weird and wonderful array of links covering every conceivable aspect of the island compiled by the indefatigable Ari Withanage.

www.yamu.lk – The long-running Yamu website (Sri Lanka's answer to *Time Out* magazine) has superb coverage of Colombo, plus patchy information on the rest of the country.

@Sheneller and @this.is.srilanka (YouTube) – Sri Lankan travel vlogger Shenelle Rodrigo's two channels have dozens of insightful videos covering destinations island-wide.

Weights and measures

Sri Lanka uses the metric system; roads are marked in kilometres.

Women travellers

Sexual harassment and assault are unfortunate realities of daily life in Sri Lanka – in one 2017 survey, for example, a staggering ninety percent of Sri Lankan women reported having experienced sexual harassment on public transport. Serious assaults are infrequent, although it's worth being aware of the potential for problems and the fact that unwanted and/or aggressive attention can happen not just on the street and in other public places, but even in situations where safety would normally be taken for granted, such as in hotels or when dealing with officials. It makes sense to avoid walking alone at night in lonely places or wearing swimwear away from the beach. You should also be aware that there have been reports in recent years of foreign women having their drinks spiked in popular resort areas, as well as hotel staff trying to enter the rooms of female guests or calling them in the middle of the night.

Language

The fact that so many Sri Lankans speak good English means that very few foreigners – including many people who live on the island – make the effort to learn any Sinhala or Tamil. Sri Lankans are therefore very unused to hearing foreigners attempting to speak their native languages and so usually respond to most attempts to do so with a mixture of incomprehension and hilarity. It's worth persevering, however, and once your listeners have got over the initial shock, they will usually respond enthusiastically to your attempts to mangle and mispronounce their rather tongue-twisting language. Many Sinhalese nouns are a simple adaptation of English words with an added *-eka*. A bus is *buseka*, a torch is *torcheka*. When in doubt or put on the spot, simply try this rule – it actually goes a long way.

Sinhala

Greetings and phrases

Yes *Ow*
No *Naa*
Hello/good day *Ayubowan*
Thank you *Istuti*
Thank you very much *Bohoma istuti*
How are you? *Kohomadhe?*
Fine *Varadak neh*
Please *Karunakerara*
What is your name? *Nama mokadhdha?*
My name is.... *Mage nama....*
OK/very good *Hari hondai*
Delicious *Hari rasai*
I don't understand *Mata terinneh neh*
Very expensive *Hari ganan*
No sugar please *Seeni netuwa*
Please stop here *Metana nawaththanna*
Where are you going? *Koheda yanna?*
Where is the hotel? *Hootale kohedha?*
Where is the station? *Stesemeta eka ko?*
What is this? *Mekeh mokadeh?*
May I telephone? *Mata call ekak ganda poluwandeh?*
How much (is this)? *(Meeka) kiyadha?*
Do you speak English? *Ingirisi dannevada?*
I don't speak Sinhala *Singhala danna naa*

Questions

What? *Mokadhdha?*
When? *Kawadadha?*
Where? *Kohedha?*
Who? *Kaudha?*
Why? *Ayi?*

Days of the week

Monday *Sanduda*
Tuesday *Angahauwada*
Wednesday *Badada*
Thursday *Brahaspathinda*
Friday *Sikurada*
Saturday *Senesurada*
Sunday *Irida*

Be aware of warning signs

Place names

Many Sinhalese place names are long but quite logical as they are nearly always a compound, so remember a few rules and you will pronounce them like a native speaker.

island *duwa*
village *gama*
river *ganga*
street *mawatha*
road *para*
city *nuwara*
stream *oya*
town *pura*
port *tota, tara*
temple *vihara*
lake *weva*
bank *bank eka*
breakfast *udee tee*
clean *pirisidu*
coffee *kopi*
dinner *paa kaama*
dirty *kilutu*
food *kaama*
hotel *hotela*
lunch *dawal kaama*
small *punchi*
pharmacy *bet sappuwa*
restaurant *apana sala*
room *kaamare*
soap *saban*
tea *tey*
this/that *meke/oya*
water *watura*

Numbers

1 *eka*
2 *deka*
3 *tuna*
4 *hatara*
5 *paha*
6 *haya*
7 *hata*
8 *ata*
9 *namaya*
10 *daaha*
11 *ekolaha*
12 *dolaha*
13 *daha tuna*
20 *vissa*
30 *tiha*
40 *hataliha*
50 *panaha*
60 *heta*
70 *heddawa*
80 *assuwa*
90 *annuwa*
100 *seeiye*
1,000 *daha*

Social media

Are you on Facebook/Instagram? *Oba Facebook-eke hari/Instagram-eke hari innawaada?*
What's your username? *Obaghe username-eka kumakdha?*
I'll add you as a friend. *Mam-ma obawa yahaluwek vidhihata add-karannam.*
I'll follow you on Instagram. *Ma-ma obawa Instagram-eke follow-karannam.*
Are you following...? *Oba .....-wa follow karanawaada?*
I'll put the pictures on Facebook/Instagram. *Mam-ma Facebook-eke/Instagram-eke pictures-dhannam.*

It's always good to know a few phrases

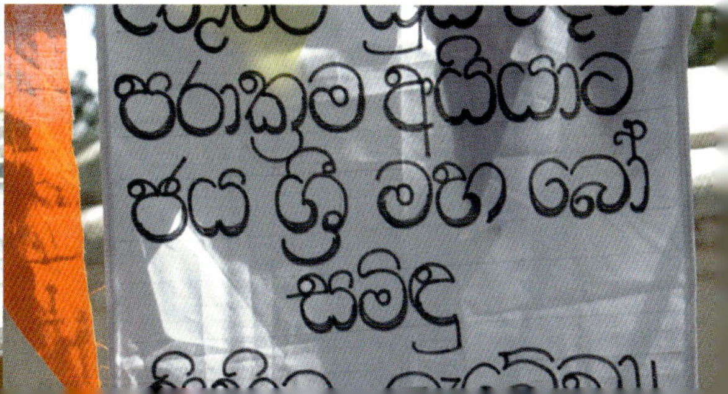

Sinhalese script

I'll tag you in the pictures. *Mam-ma oyaawa pictures-wala tag-karannam.*

Tamil

Basics

Hello *Vanakkam*
Goodbye *Poyvituvarukiren* (Reply *Poyvituvarungal)*
Yes *Amam*
No *Illai*
Perhaps *Oruvelai*
Thank you *Nandri*
How are you? *Celakkiyama?*
What is your name? *Ungal peyar yenna?*
My name is (John/Jane) *Yen peyar (John/Jane)*
Where is the (hotel)? *(Hotel) yenge?*
What is this/that? *Idu/Adu yenna?*
What is the price? *Yenna vilai?*
That is very expensive *Anda vilai mikavum adikum*
I want (coffee) *(Kapi) Vendum*
I like (dosa) *(Dosai) Pudikkum*
Is it possible? *Mudiyuma?*
I don't understand *Puriyadu*
Enough *Podum*

Useful words

Toilet *Tailet*
Train *Rayil*
Bed *Kattil*
Room *Arai*
Bedroom *Patukkai arai*
Sari *Pudavai*
Dhoti *Vesti*
Towel *Tundu*
Sandals *Ceruppu*
Money *Punam*
Temple *Kovil*

Verbs

Come! (imperative) *Varungal*
Go (imperative) *Pongal*
Stop (imperative) *Nillungal*
Sleep *Tungu*
Eat *Sappidu*
Drink *Kudi*
Buy *Vangu*
Pay (money) *Punam kodu* (literally 'give money')
See *Par*
Wash (clothes) *Tuvai*
Wash (yourself) *Kazhavu*

Questions

How? *Yeppadi?*
What? *Yenna?*
Who? *Yar?*
Why? *Yen?*
Where? *Yenge?*
When? *Yeppodu?*
How much? *Yettanai/Yevvalavu?*

Days of the week

Monday *Tingal*
Tuesday *Cevvay*
Wednesday *Putam*
Thursday *Viyazhan*
Friday *Velli*
Saturday *Ceni*
Sunday *Nayiri*
Today *Inraikku*
Week *Varam*
Month *Matam*
Year *Varutam*

A local on Negombo beach

Numbers

1 *onru*
2 *irandu*
3 *munru*
4 *nanku*
5 *aindu*
6 *aru*
7 *yezhu*
8 *yettu*
9 *onpadu*
10 *pattu*
11 *patinonru*
12 *pannirandu*
20 *irupadu*
30 *muppadu*
40 *rarpadu*
50 *aimpadu*
60 *arupadu*
70 *alupadu*
80 *yenpadu*
90 *tonnuru*
100 *nuru*
100,000 *latcam*
10,000,000 *kodi*

Health

I am sick (vomiting) *Utampu cariyillai irukkiradu*
I have a pain *Vali irukkiradu*
I have diarrhoea *irrukkiradu*
Doctor *Taktar*
Help! *Utavi cey!*

Food

Food *Sappadu*
Water *Tunnir*
Rice *Sadum*
Fruit *Puzham*
Vegetables *Kaykuri*
Milk *Pal*
Coconut *Tengay*
Mango *Mampazham*
Banana *Valaippazham*
Coffee *Kapi*
Tea *Ti*
Steamed rice cakes *Idli*
Pancake made from fermented dough *Dosai*
Thin, spicy soup, usually with a tamarind base *Vadai Rasam*
Dry vegetable curry *Poriyal*
Chicken curry *Kolikarri*
Lamb curry *Attukkari*
Sweet festival dish *Payasam*
Mils 'Meals', similar to a North Indian thali (a selection of different small dishes), traditionally served on a banana leaf

Social media

Are you on Facebook/Instagram? *Neenga Facebook-il allathu/ Instagram-il irrukireerkala?*
What's your username? *Ungal paeyanar payar enna?*
I'll add you as a friend. *Naan ungalai nanbaraaha saerkiraen.*
I'll follow you on Instagram. *Naan ungalai twitter-il pinpatuvaen.*
Are you following...? *Neengal... ai pinpatureerkalaa?*
I'll put the pictures on Facebook/ Instagram. *Naan Facebook-il/ Instagram-il padangalai pordhukiraen.*
I'll tag you in the pictures. *Naan padangalil ungalai tag-panuvaen.*

Universal language

Many signs are also in English

Books and Film

With its fascinating history and recent political tumult, Sri Lanka has inspired many authors of both fiction and non-fiction There is also a small but strong Sinhala-language film industry producing films for local cinemas, while a fair number of international movies have also been shot in the country.

Books

Fiction

Colpetty People Ashok Ferrey. Entertaining vignettes, full of comedy and social insights, by one of Sri Lanka's leading short story writers.

Funny Boy Shyam Selvadurai. Touching novel chronicling the life of a young Tamil boy growing up in Colombo in the years leading up to the civil war.

The Hamilton Case Michelle de Kretser. Cleverly plotted and beautifully written whodunnit set in the British colonial era and chronicling the life and career of lawyer Sam Obeysekere and his chance involvement in the murder of a British planter.

The Jam Fruit Tree trilogy Carl Muller. This popular trilogy of novels *(The Jam Fruit Tree, Yakada Yaka* and *Once Upon A Tender Time)* describes the comic misadventures of the slow-witted Von Bloss family, lower-class railway Burghers living in Colombo and Kandy.

Reef Romesh Gunesekera. Shortlisted for the Booker Prize, this strangely captivating novel describes the relationship between Sri Lankan marine biologist Mister Salgado and his young houseboy cook Triton, giving a distinctive flavour of the island's cooking and history.

Running in the Family Michael Ondaatje. This superbly written memoir describes the maverick lives, loves and extended bouts of drunkenness of Ondaajte's Sri Lankan Burgher relatives, beautifully capturing the eccentric flavour of a vanished era. Ondaatje's other Sri Lankan book, the novel *Anil's Ghost*, is altogether darker, offering a lightly fictionalised account of the island during the civil war and JVP insurrection.

The Seven Moons of Maali Almeida Shehan Karunatilaka. Booker Prize-winning novel relating the phantasmagorical story of murdered Sri Lankan war photographer Maali Almeida as he goes hunting through the afterlife for his killers. Karunatilaka's gloriously madcap, cricket-obsessed first novel, *Chinaman*, is also essential Sri Lankan reading, following a dying sportswriter's attempts to hunt down mysterious spin bowler Pradeep S. Mathew.

The Village in the Jungle Leonard Woolf. Superbly depressing tale of life in the backwaters of southern

Sri Lankan author Michael Ondaatje

Sri Lanka – a place Woolf knew intimately from his work as a colonial administrator in Hambantota.

History and travel

A Long Watch: War, Captivity and Return in Sri Lanka. Ajith Boyagoda and Sunila Galappatti. Eloquent account by former naval office Ajith Boyagoda of his eight years as a captive of the LTTE – and one which bravely challenges many Sinhalese prejudices and preconceptions about the hated Tigers.
A History of Sri Lanka K.M. de Silva. The best history of Sri Lanka, presenting an intelligent overview of the island's political and cultural history.
Only Man Is Vile William McGowan. Superbly insightful and disquieting account of war-torn Sri Lanka in the late 1980s during its twin struggles against the Tamil Tigers and JVP.
Wave: A Memoir of Life After the Tsunami Sonali Deraniyagala. Written by a tsunami survivor who lost her husband, parents and two young children in the disaster, this memoir is courageously understated and probably the nearest any of us will get to understanding such unimaginable grief.

Art and architecture

The Architecture of an Island Barbara Sansoni, Ronald Lewcock and Laki Senanayake. Beautiful line drawings and descriptions of 95 classic Sri Lankan structures, from chicken coops to colonial cathedrals.
Geoffrey Bawa: The Complete Works David Robson. Sumptuous volume covering the work of Sri Lanka's foremost modern architect, with insightful text and superb photography.

Specialist guides

A Field Guide to the Birds of Sri Lanka John Harrison and Tim Worfolk. The definitive field handbook to the island's immense ornithological riches.
A Photographic Guide to the Birds of Sri Lanka Gehan de Silva Wijeyeratne et al. Excellent little pocket guide with good photographs of all Sri Lankan bird species along with useful accompanying notes.

Film

A Common Man (2013). Sir Ben Kingsley stars in this remake of an Indian film about an anonymous man planting bombs across Colombo and using this threat as leverage to have four notorious terrorists released from prison.
The Bridge on the River Kwai (1957). Classic war film starring William Holden and Alec Guinness, set in Thailand but actually shot in Sri Lanka around Kitulgala.
Indiana Jones and the Temple of Doom (1984). This second in the blockbusting franchise was partly shot on location around Kandy, after the Indian authorities refused permission to Steven Spielberg and co. on the grounds of finding the material offensive to India and Hinduism.

Alec Guinness in 'The Bridge on the River Kwai'

About This Book

The Rough Guides Walks & Tours series helps you discover the world's most exciting destinations through our expert-curated trip plans: a range of walks and tours designed to suit all budgets, interests and trip lengths. These walks, driving tours and site excursions cover the destination's most quintessential attractions as well as a range of lesser-known sights, while food and drink stops for refreshments en route are highlighted in boxes. If you're not sure which walk to pick, our Best walks & tours for... feature suggests which ones work best for particular interests. The introduction provides a destination overview, while the directory supports the walks and tours with all the essential information you need, as well as our pick of where to stay while you are there and select restaurant listings, to complement the more low-key options given in the trip plans.

About the authors

This edition was updated by Gavin Thomas. Gavin has been visiting Sri Lanka for over twenty years, travelling to every corner of the country and seeing at first hand the varying effects of civil war, tsunami, peacetime reconstruction and the economic crisis. He is also the author of the **Rough Guide to Sri Lanka**.

Help us update

We've gone to a lot of effort to ensure that this edition of the **Rough Guides Walks & Tours Sri Lanka** is accurate and up-to-date. However, things change – places get "discovered", new gems open up, restaurants and rooms raise prices or lower standards. If you feel we've got it wrong or left something out, we'd like to know, and if you can remember the address, the website, whether or not it was free to enter – so much the better.

Please send your comments with the subject line "**Rough Guides Walks & Tours Sri Lanka Update**" to mail@uk.roughguides.com. We'll acknowledge all contributions and send a copy of the next edition (or any other Rough Guide if you prefer) for the very best emails.

Credits

Rough Guides Walks & Tours Sri Lanka
Editor: Sarah Clark
Author: Gavin Thomas
Picture Editor: Tom Smyth
Cartography: Katie Bennett
Layout: Ankur Guha
Production Operations Manager: Katie Bennett
Publishing Technology Manager: Rebeka Davies
Head of Publishing: Sarah Clark
Photo credits: Bigstock 6B, 18/19; Casa Colombo 88; Chaaya Hotels & Resorts 96L; Columbia Pictures 121; Dreamstime 34, 54/55, 59R; Fotolia 50, 102; Heritance Hotels 93R, 94L, 96L; Indi Samarajiva 22, 23B, 37R, 56T, 110, 110/111, 113; iStock 4BL, 4BR, 17T, 38, 46/47, 103R; Jetwing Hotels 16, 89, 90, 91, 92, 92/93; Leonardo 94L, 94/95, 96/97; Marcus Wilson Smith/Apa Publications 102/103; Mount Lavinia Hotel 98, 99R; Shutterstock 1, 4T, 6ML, 7M, 8/9, 10, 11B, 11T, 12L, 12/13, 13, 14, 14/15, 15R, 19R, 26, 27T, 28/29, 30, 31, 32, 33, 35, 42, 45R, 44/45, 47R, 48, 52, 56B, 57R, 56/57, 58, 58/59, 60, 61, 69R, 72, 74, 76, 77, 78, 79, 80, 81, 82, 83, 84, 85, 86/87, 98/99, 100, 101, 120; Sri Lanka Tourism 6TL, 17B, 18, 24L, 25R, 24/25; Sylvaine Poitau/Apa Publications 4MR, 6MC, 7T, 7MR, 7MR, 20, 21R, 20/21, 23T, 27B, 36, 36/37, 39, 40, 41, 43, 44, 46, 49, 51R, 50/51, 53, 62L, 63R, 62/63, 64, 65R, 64/65, 66, 67, 68, 68/69, 70, 71, 73, 74/75, 75R, 104, 105, 106, 106/107, 107R, 108, 109, 111R, 112, 114/115, 116L, 116/117, 117R, 118, 118/119, 119R
Cover credits: Lion's paws pathway on Sigiriya Rock
Shutterstock

Printed in Czech Republic

This book was produced using **Typefi** automated publishing software.

First edition 2024

Distribution

UK, Ireland and Europe
Apa Publications (UK) Ltd
sales@roughguides.com
United States and Canada
Ingram Publisher Services
ips@ingramcontent.com
Australia and New Zealand
Booktopia
retailer@booktopia.com.au
Worldwide
Apa Publications (UK) Ltd
sales@roughguides.com

Special Sales, Content Licensing and CoPublishing

Rough Guides can be purchased in bulk quantities at discounted prices. We can create special editions, personalised jackets and corporate imprints tailored to your needs.
sales@roughguides.com
http://roughguides.com

Index

T

U

V

W

Y

MAP LEGEND

- Start of tour
- Tour & route direction
- Recommended sight
- Recommended restaurant/café
- Place of interest
- Tourist information
- Statue/monument
- Buddhist/Hindu temple
- Main post office
- Main bus station
- Ancient Site
- Ferry route
- National park boundry
- Province boundary
- District boundary
- Park
- Important building
- Hotel
- Transport hub
- Shopping / market
- Pedestrian area
- Urban area
- Marsh